W9-AOL-255

THE FORM OF A SERVANT

THE
FORM
OF A
SERVANT

A Historical Analysis of the Kenotic Motif

by

Donald G. Dawe

Philadelphia

THE WESTMINSTER PRESS

LIBRARY OF CONGRESS CATALOG CARD NO. 64–10064

PUBLISHED BY THE WESTMINSTER PRESS ®

PHILADELPHIA 7, PENNSYLVANIA

PRINTED IN THE UNITED STATES OF AMERICA

To my parents,
through whom I first came to know Him
who was in the Form of a Servant

Contents

Preface

The purpose of this book is twofold. It is to explore historically the kenotic tradition in Christological thought. In this tradition the incarnation is interpreted as an act of divine self-emptying or limitation. Further, it is an effort to apply the insights of this tradition to building a contemporary Christology. Whenever kenotic Christologies are mentioned, the most usual association is with a particular school of Christology that flourished on the Continent and then in the English-speaking world during the nineteenth and early twentieth centuries. Viewed in this way, a study of the kenotic Christologies can only be a chapter in the history of the mediating theology of the recent past. But to approach the kenotic tradition this way is to overlook both its antiquity and its ubiquity. The kenotic motif is found on the earliest levels of Christian tradition, probably antedating its appearances in the Pauline epistles. The motif has played a part in every age of Christian thought and life. The theme of divine self-emptying is found not only in works of theology but in liturgies, sermons, and manuals of ascetic piety. The church as the servant people has been faced in every age with the image of its Servant Lord. We look to this image again not simply as an exercise in historical reflection and scholarship but as a source of fresh insight for Christology today.

Christological thought in our day is beset by a variety of problems. Some of these problems derive from unresolved, and probably unresolvable, conflicts on the earliest levels of Chris-

9

tological reflection. The problem of intellectually conceiving the being of the God-man is a perennial feature of Christian theology. It stems from the basic Christian confession of Jesus Christ as Lord. In every age the church has struggled to make this confession intelligible to the mind of its time. How can we speak of one who is both human and divine? In the early centuries of its life the Christian church wrestled with this problem in terms of the thought world of Greco-Roman antiquity. Out of this struggle came the ecumenical creeds and the patristic theology which defined Christological orthodoxy until modern times. Yet even this great movement of thought failed to give rational coherence to the Christological affirmations. It served to rule out certain heresies. And it provided the major intellectual framework within which Christological reflection was conducted. The basic problem of conceiving the divine and human natures in Jesus Christ remains as critical a one for our own time as it was for antiquity. We can transcend the framework of the patristic theology by historical analysis, but we cannot avoid the questions faced by the fathers in past centuries.

In addition to what we might call the " classical " Christological problems, contemporary theology is faced by another set of problems that are uniquely modern in origin. These problems stem from the new religious and philosophical consciousness which has arisen since the Enlightenment of the eighteenth century. The church has been forced to rethink its Christology in a most radical way because of the new awareness of history and understanding of personality that is basic for all contemporary thought. Historical scholarship has given us a new and clearer picture of Jesus as a man of the first century; and from this picture has come the concern for conceiving Jesus' mental, emotional, and spiritual life. Could this new picture of Jesus' psychical life as that of a first-century Jew be related in any way to the traditional affirmations of his divinity? How is the " Jesus of history " related to the " Christ of faith "?

The contemporary importance of the kenotic motif for Christology lies in the unique way in which it is related to both the classical and the modern Christological problems. The kenotic motif embraces the problems of the divine-human being and the divine-human consciousness. It is a motif that illumines the basic issues that face Christology today. As such, the kenotic motif is a basic building block in the reconstruction of Christology.

I wish to express thanks to my colleagues at Union Theological Seminary and Macalester College for their guidance on technical matters and their support and encouragement while I was working on the book. My particular thanks go to Macalester College for a generous grant from the Wallace Research Fund to complete my research and writing. Personal thanks are due Mrs. Gordon Sprain, whose skill and concern brought the manuscript into final form.

D. G. D.

Macalester College
St. Paul, Minnesota

Chapter I

A New Look at an Ancient Teaching

THE METHOD OF APPROACH

Introduction

Basic to Christian faith is the belief in the divine self-emptying or condescension in Christ for the redemption of men. According to Christian faith, God in his creation and redemption of the world accepted the limitations of finitude upon his own person. In the words of the New Testament, God had "emptied himself, taking the form of a servant." God accepted the limitations of human life, its suffering and death, but in doing this, he had not ceased being God. God the Creator had chosen to live as a creature. God, who in his eternity stood forever beyond the limitations of human life, had fully accepted these limitations. The Creator had come under the power of his creation. This the Christian faith has declared in various ways from its beginning. And men have struggled to understand this bold and unique belief throughout Christian history. Despite these struggles, this belief has most often been misunderstood. Yet the proper understanding of it is imperative because it leads us to the very core of what is unique in Christian faith.

All early Christian confessions witnessed to the faith that God had condescended by a free act of self-limitation to live in and through a fully human being, Jesus of Nazareth. In that life, Christians said, God had given his saving revelation to mankind. God revealed himself not by giving to a chosen, spiritual elite a mystical vision of his glory. God was not to be viewed like a statue long veiled that is then revealed but remains unchanged in the revelation. Rather, in his saving revelation God emptied himself, laying aside his glory to take up a human life. God shared the common lot of humanity and so made himself known to common humanity. God, who was believed to dwell forever beyond all change and passion, had freely entered the change and passion of human life for its redemption.

This faith in God's self-limitation is first clearly expressed in the New Testament. A hymn about Christ pointing back to the earliest Christian traditions unfolds this faith:

Though he was in the form of God, [he] did not count equality with God a thing to be grasped, but emptied himself, taking the form of a servant, being born in the likeness of men. And being found in human form he humbled himself and became obedient unto death, even death on a cross.

Therefore God has highly exalted him and bestowed on him the name which is above every name, that at the name of Jesus every knee should bow, in heaven and on earth and under the earth, and every tongue confess that Jesus Christ is Lord, to the glory of God the Father. (Phil. 2:6-11, RSV.)

Here the contrast is placed clearly in view. The Christ who was " in the form of God " had taken the " form of a servant." He who had shared the glories of the divine life now freely shared the ignominy of human life. The One destined to be Lord of all was also the Servant of all.

This belief in God's self-emptying in Christ is the inevitable outcome of the religious situation pictured in the New Testament. On the one hand, there is the abiding faith of Israel in the one God. He is the God of unapproachable majesty who had spoken through prophets and whose power had shaped the destiny of the people of God. On the other hand, there is the faith that this same God had encountered men in a new way. The prologue to Hebrews describes this contrast: " In many and various ways God spoke of old to our fathers by the prophets; but in these last days he has spoken to us by a Son."

(Heb. 1:1-2a.) God was known to be personally present in Jesus of Nazareth who had lived amid the limitations, sufferings, and death that afflict every man. This Jesus was the Christ who had shared the glory of the Godhead. Yet he was also the One who died on the cross.

The contrast between these two fundamental assertions of faith inevitably raised a question that has been asked in one form or another since the earliest days of Christianity. How can these two opposite modes of existence be attributed to one person? How can one who shares the life of God also share the life of man? The answer of Christian faith to this question took explicit form in Phil. 2:6. The Christ had "emptied himself [*heauton ekenōsen*], taking the form of a servant." The technical name given to this answer of faith derives from the Greek word translated "emptied" — *kenoō*. It is called the kenosis. It is a belief in the divine self-emptying. Put very simply, it is the belief that in Jesus Christ, God limited himself in some aspect of his being or person to live a human life.

The audacity of this belief in the divine kenosis has often been lost by long familiarity with it. The familiar phrases "he emptied himself, taking the form of a servant," "though he was rich, yet for your sake he became poor," have come to seem commonplace. Yet this belief in the divine self-emptying epitomizes the radically new message of Christian faith about God and his relation to man. The transformation that the kenosis theme brought about in the traditional ideas of God and religion in the ancient world is easily forgotten because it has long been assimilated into accepted doctrinal formulas. The ancient Roman skeptic Celsus caught both the uniqueness and the centrality of the kenosis doctrine in the Christian understanding of God. He saw the final proof of the inherent absurdity of Christianity in its belief that God, an Immortal, living forever beyond change, had come down and accepted the changes and sufferings of mortal life. Yet this belief in God's free acceptance of change is the very core of the Christian message.

It is the key assertion that reduced Christianity to intellectual folly.

I make no new statement, but say what has long been settled. God is good, and beautiful, and blessed, and that in the best and most beautiful degree. But if He comes down among men, He must undergo a change, and a change from good to evil, from beauty to ugliness, from happiness to misery, and from best to worst. Who then would make choice of such a change? (Origen, *Against Celsus* IV. 14.)

Celsus' argument rests upon a typically Greek conception of God. From this point of view, to talk of a divine kenosis is to speak pure nonsense. In the Greek conception the essence of divinity was existence beyond change and suffering and death. To say that God had accepted these limitations into his own being was akin to saying that God was no longer God.

Similarly, to the Jewish piety of late antiquity the notion of the utterly transcendent One, whose very name was too holy to be spoken, living in and through Jesus of Nazareth was a blasphemy. Yet such was the faith of the earliest believers in Jesus Christ. It was this belief that made Christianity " to the Jews a stumblingblock, to the Greeks foolishness." These ancient critics of Christianity saw belief in the divine self-emptying as the very heart of the faith. They have seen more clearly than have many Christians the way in which the doctrine of the divine self-emptying in Christ embraces what is unique about Christianity.

Men have long pondered belief in the divine kenosis to unlock its mysteries. The history of the kenosis idea in Christian thought is one marked by a curious mixture of insight and misunderstanding. Theologians have tried to explain it in terms of many different patterns of thought about God. But they have discovered that this idea fits into none of their patterns fully. The kenosis idea cuts across all the established lines of thought about God. Throughout the history of Christian thought this idea has reasserted itself creatively in the development of Christology, of the doctrine of God, and of the Chris-

tian life. Yet the kenosis idea has seldom been properly understood in terms of itself. The purpose of this study is to analyze
the ways in which the kenosis idea has been interpreted. Out
of an evaluation of both its uses and abuses in the past an
appraisal will be made of its place in the modern restatement
of Christian faith.

The Scope of the Kenosis Theme

From the earliest formulations of the kenosis theme in the
New Testament it is clear that belief in the divine self-emptying is not an isolated affirmation of Christian faith. The divine
kenosis is the key to the whole drama of human salvation. It
touches on questions of ethics and church life as well as theology. The earliest explicit formulations of kenosis, Phil. 2:5-11
and II Cor. 8:9, illustrate the richness and inclusiveness of the
motif. In Philippians, Paul used the moral appeal of Christ's
self-emptying as the basis for an admonition to humility. Paul
holds before the Philippian congregation Christ's supreme example of humility in leaving the heavenly realm to dwell " in
the form of a servant." Similarly, in Second Corinthians the
theme of Christ's kenosis is used as the basis of an appeal for
liberality in giving to the poor of the Jerusalem church. In
these contexts the appeal of the motif is of a practical, ethical
sort. The moral appeal of God's free self-giving is the motiva-
tion for the life of self-giving love for the Christian. God's free
self-giving, his kenosis, describes the pattern of life for the
Christian. At the same time the basis of this moral appeal —
Christ's own act of self-emptying — was a profound statement
of Christology destined to shape and reshape Christian thought
for generations to come. Kenosis is a way of describing the
divine being and the divine action in Christ. It is a motif in
worship, ethics, and theology.

The kenosis motif is such a basic and inclusive theme in
Christian faith that it has the power of throwing into clear
and dramatic focus the great issues in the history of doctrine.
The kenosis motif illumines the question of the freedom and

unchangeableness of God. It asks how God can both empty himself and remain unchanged. The kenosis motif involves the question of how the members of the Trinity are related. It raises to the critical point the question of the significance of Jesus' historical life. How can a life be really human if that life is in some sense still a divine life? Kenosis illumines the meaning of the life of faith and obedience of the Christian believer. As has already been seen in the earliest New Testament formulations, the kenosis theme describes the quality of life the believer receives from God. The kenosis is not only a description of the Servant Lord, but it involves the servant people.

Kenosis is a theme expressed through Christian literature in every age. From an early Christian hymn in Philippians to a sermon by Origen, from a treatise of Tertullian to the hymns of Wesley, from the homilies of Gregory of Nazianzus to the meditations of Zinzendorf, from the mystical writings of Bernard to the ontology of Hegel, from the sermons of Luther to the theology of Barth, the kenosis motif is found. Treatments of the doctrines of God, of Christ, and of the Christian life have all made reference to the divine self-emptying. Yet the importance of the kenosis motif has often been overlooked by historians of doctrine. Consideration of the kenosis has usually been limited to New Testament studies or, at most, extended to cover the so-called kenotic Christologies formulated during the nineteenth and early twentieth centuries. Whenever the kenosis idea is mentioned, the names of Gottfried Thomasius, Bishop Gore, or P. T. Forsyth, and others come to mind. These men sought to build a modern Christology on the basis of the kenosis motif. But, as is well known, these Christologies have since come under sharp criticism and are no longer influential. For many, this has meant that any form of kenosis doctrine is branded as passé or, at best, relegated to a corner in New Testament history where it will not affect theological thinking. To do this is to place a limitation on the study of the kenosis motif that is unnecessary and misleading. For kenosis is not simply a matter of certain Christologies formulated by theologians of the recent past. Nor is it simply a question of some isolated New Testament passages. Instead, the kenotic theme expresses a basic faith of the church: the faith that in Christ, God limited himself and lived a fully human life. Kenosis expresses the faith that God is free to be our God in the fullest sense. He is free to live the life of man and yet be Lord of all. This is no isolated affirmation. It touches the wellspring of Christian faith.

Kenosis — Motif and Doctrine

In the face of a theme so all-embracing and a literature so extensive, it is necessary to make certain distinctions and to define terms. The kenosis idea has taken many forms throughout its history. The distinctions between these forms requires closer analysis before the significance of kenosis can be properly appreciated and its constructive possibilities for modern theology comprehended. The term used thus far to describe the kenosis theme in Christian faith, particularly as found in the New Testament, has been the word "motif." Belief in the divine self-emptying is a basic motif of Christian faith. The aim of this study is to analyze the uses of this motif in the development of specific Christian doctrines. To carry out such an analysis, it is necessary to define the terms "motif" and "doctrine."

The term "motif" was introduced into modern theological study and historical research by Anders Nygren. However, the term takes its basic definition from the realm of literary and artistic analysis and criticism. A motif in a work of art is the salient feature of a work, particularly its theme or dominant feature. It is a recurrent theme that gives meaning to the whole. The motif integrates the many complex features of a work and in turn is evidenced throughout the various parts of a work. Proceeding from this artistic and literary definition of the term, Nygren particularized it for use in theological study. He especially focused attention on two features of the motif that are relevant here: (1) To qualify as a motif, an idea must be of fundamental or categorical significance. A motif in a body of religious thought is an answer to a basic or recurring question. Hence, there are only a few motifs that characterize a subject. (2) Because of its nature as a theme of fundamental or underlying significance, the motif can be expressed through a variety of means. To say that a motif is the answer to a fundamental question or concern does not mean it must take the form of an abstract propositional statement. It may equally well be a general underlying sentiment expressed through a variety of assertions. A motif by its very nature as a broad assertion can be expressed through various systems of thought. But the motif retains its basic character within whatever particular formulation it is given. The motif is always more basic and more general than any of the particular doctrines or formulas that express it.

In the light of this definition, kenosis can be seen as a motif of Christian faith. The kenosis motif is the answer given by Christian faith to the basic question: How does God redeem the world? The answer given by Christian faith is that in Jesus Christ, God had freely and totally given himself. God had limited himself and shared in human life. God had accepted into his own being the very limitations of life that held men in bondage. But God had triumphed over them. In the light of the salvation given in Christ, men realized that God does not redeem by overpowering might or by a sheer unveiling of his glory. In stark opposition to all human attempts at salvation by self-assertions, the characteristic saving act of God is one of self-emptying. Kenosis is a basic motif or characteristic of the Christian faith in God. It expresses a new conception of God and his redemption of mankind through Christ.

Already in the New Testament the many possible orientations of this motif are evident. Paul related the kenosis motif to ethical problems at Philippi and Corinth. Yet he made the ethical appeal on the basis of a Christological doctrine. Bernard of Clairvaux illumined the problems of mystical piety by reference to kenosis. Later, Luther and Zinzendorf derived personal assurance in the face of guilt and doubt by reference to the kenotic motif. Thomasius and Forsyth sought to build a Christology intelligible to the modern world on the basis of the kenosis. Karl Barth sees in the kenosis motif an important building block in his doctrine of God. The kenosis motif has found expression in many forms and through systems of thought sharply differentiated from one another. Yet in all these settings the uniquely characteristic faith in God's self-emptying remains constant. It is constant because it is a basic motif of the faith that underlies and informs all Christian theology.

Throughout its history the kenosis motif has come to expression in particular doctrines or theological formulas. In contrast to the motif, doctrines are propositional statements employing various philosophical, religious, and commonsense language forms. Doctrines are the means by which a faith is given verbal expression and intellectual structure. By their very nature as verbal forms based on a process of intellectual reflection and abstraction, doctrines never fully express faith. Rather, doctrines provide perspectives and guides to the meaning of faith. They are the means by which a religious faith is related critically to its sources in Scripture and tradition. Doctrine also provides a way of relating religious faith to the apprehensions of truth in other human endeavors and intellectual disciplines.

Religious doctrines seek to give an ordered or systematic statement to the faith that underlies them. The formulation of doctrine is a means of bringing order into the complex of metaphors, myths, and historical accounts that constitute the language of Scripture and tradition. In this process of systematic statement the basic motifs of faith undergo a change. They are no longer expressed in the concrete metaphors or mythological language of firsthand religious experience. They take on the abstract, conceptual language forms of the thought world in which they are being expressed. This is very evident in the development of the kenosis theme in the history of Christianity. In the early church the kenosis motif was expressed in the concrete pictorial language of Jewish apocalyptic and Hellenistic

Gnostic mythology. Already in the second century the church fathers were struggling to express it within the thought patterns of Greek philosophy. In the Middle Ages the place of the kenosis motif was determined by a Platonic or Aristotelian conception of being. Among the nineteenth-century Germans who used the kenosis motif in their Christologies the philosophical conceptions of romantic idealism were employed. These various forms of kenosis doctrine are approaches to the common motif of Christian faith that underlies them — the belief in God's free self-emptying. The various kenotic doctrines throughout the ages differ in their specific forms and orientations because they reflect differing philosophical and religious outlooks. They are united in expressing a common belief in God's self-emptying.

This distinction between kenosis as a motif of Christian faith and the various kenotic doctrines that express that faith serves a dual purpose: (1) The distinction illustrates the breadth and vitality of the kenosis idea. It is not a conception limited to one time or place in the history of the church. It is a broad, recurring theme that is expressed in differing ways throughout the history of Christianity. (2) This distinction is made to establish the lines of historical continuity between the great kenotic doctrines that have appeared in Christian history, particularly those of modern times, and their roots in the New Testament and the fathers. As Frederic Loofs rightly perceived in his historical analysis of the kenotic idea in Christian thought, the continuity between the modern kenotic doctrines and those found in the New Testament and the fathers is not simple and direct.[1] The historical, psychological, and philosophical concerns, for example, that shaped all the modern kenotic doctrines were largely foreign to the kenotic formulas of the early church. It would be misleading to think there had been a direct and gradual evolution of earlier kenotic doctrines into the later ones. In fact, at times there was no formal kenotic doctrine as such. Rather, the history of kenosis is to be traced in the reassertion of a basic motif of faith in different forms. Sometimes it is found in theological formulas, some-times in sermons, liturgies, or prayers. The continuity is that of a basic aspect of Christian faith rather than that of specific doctrinal formulas.

The aim of this study is to understand the ways in which the kenosis motif was expressed through the various religious and philosophical ideas that have shaped Christian thought. Two ages in the history of Christianity have been particularly crucial for the interpretation of the kenosis motif. The first was that age when the church sought to express its faith in the language and thought forms of Greco-Roman antiquity. This is the age of transition from the Christianity of the New Testa-ment church to that of the fathers and the Ecumenical Coun-cils of the fourth and fifth centuries. Here were set the domi-nant features for understanding the kenosis motif that held sway until the rise of the modern religious consciousness in the eighteenth and nineteenth centuries.

The second crucial age in determining the meaning of keno-sis was that time in the nineteenth century when the modern view of man and the world necessitated a restatement of Chris-tian faith. This reinterpretation of the faith in the light of the modern world view is a task in which the church is still in-volved. The basic changes in modes of understanding and cate-gories of thought in the modern world have reopened the ques-tion of the kenosis motif and its importance in a dramatic way. The new ways of psychological and historical thought opened to men in the modern world have made possible an exploration of the richness of the kenosis motif unknown in the past. And the rise of dynamic and personalistic categories in ontology have opened a new and deeper way of expressing the divine kenosis.[2] The study of the kenosis motif and its restatement in contemporary terms throws into sharp focus the complex in-teraction of Christian faith and modern intellect. Out of this interaction a fresh statement of the kenosis motif can become a reality.

The major procedural assumption of this historical study

and restatement of the kenosis motif is that it is possible " to overcome history by history." These famous words of Ernst Troeltsch describe the function of historical study in reaching a modern, constructive statement of Christian faith. " To overcome history by history " means that through continuing historical analysis it is possible to overcome the failures and limitations of past embodiments of truth and to glimpse afresh the realities they sought to express. As it becomes possible through historical study to understand the religious and intellectual setting out of which a given formulation of Christian doctrine arose, then the truth it embodied can be apprehended anew. The need for such a historical analysis of the kenosis motif is clear. For to a remarkable degree, thought about the kenosis has been effectively stymied because of the limitations inherited from the kenotic formulas of the past. The kenotic doctrines of the church fathers and of certain theologians of the recent past have so completely dominated thought about kenosis that new developments have not been possible. But through historical understanding of these formulas the realities to which they witness may be more clearly seen.

The order of historical study will be chronological, starting with the New Testament and proceeding to the present time. However, some exceptions must be made to this pattern in order to make certain parts more intelligible. The development of the modern kenotic Christologies in Germany and later in the English-speaking world during the past century constitute a historical landmark to which reference must often be made. The theologians and Bible scholars who formulated these Christologies undertook extensive historical studies that changed long-standing patterns of thought. The originator and chief figure in this group was Gottfried Thomasius, whose epoch-making work first appeared in 1845. His work was followed on the Continent by that of August Ebrard, Bishop Martensen, and later in the English-speaking world by Bishop Gore, P. T. Forsyth, and H. R. Mackintosh. In addition to these theologians, certain Bible scholars such as Frederic Godet and Bishop

Lightfoot made important studies of the roots of the kenosis idea in New Testament thought. The work of these and other scholars of the recent past basically changed the ways of approaching the kenosis motif. Although many of their formulations of the kenosis are beset by serious limitations, they did challenge the traditional understanding of the kenosis that had long been established. Because of their basic importance, they will be mentioned in the section on the New Testament and the church fathers, although they do not come on the scene until centuries later.

Chapter II

The Form of God — The Form of a Servant

THE KENOTIC MOTIF IN THE NEW TESTAMENT

The Question of Method

The problem of interpreting the importance of the kenotic motif in the New Testament is of almost monumental proportions. The literature that deals with the subject is immense in scope, and the conflicts of opinion are many. So a preliminary look at the method of approach is necessary before moving into the midst of the problem itself. The line of argument to be followed in studying the kenotic motif in the New Testament may be stated in general.

First, attention must be given the extent and importance of the kenotic motif for the New Testament as a whole. How widespread is the kenosis theme? What is its importance in the message of the New Testament?

Secondly, the pursuit of this question leads to a consideration of the specific kenotic formulas, especially Phil. 2:5-11, the *locus classicus* of all kenotic thought. Because of the basic importance of this passage, its interpretation is studied in both its historical and modern forms. Attention must be given to the traditional exegesis of the Philippian passage, for to a remarkable degree the approach to the kenosis idea by Christian thinkers has been shaped by this interpretation to the present day. The revolutionary import of modern critico-historical study for the kenotic motif becomes intelligible only against the background of its historical development.

Thirdly, against the background of the history of its exegesis a detailed study is made of the Philippian passage in relation to its background in the ancient world. Consideration is given to its literary form, its unique key words, and its parallels in the religious literature of the time. Finally, with the understanding of kenosis given in Philippians, it is then possible to return to the question of the importance of the motif for the New Testament as a whole.

The Importance of Kenosis

The question of the exact extent and importance of the kenotic motif for New Testament thought is a vexed one. There have been scholars who have argued that the whole of the New Testament bears witness to the kenotic motif. And there have been those who have pointed to the limited number of specific kenotic formulas in the New Testament. These scholars have given the kenosis theme only a limited importance as one of several New Testament Christologies. Both these observations illumine part of the truth. For the kenosis theme is both a general motif found in the revelation to which the New Testament witnesses, and it is a specific doctrine of Christology formulated in certain parts of the New Testament itself. Thus in a study of the place of kenosis in the New Testament, an alternation of attention is necessary between the specific kenotic formulas, such as Phil. 2:5-11, and the way in which these formulas illumine the whole of the New Testament message. To understand the place of the kenosis motif properly, both its general importance and its specific formulations must be taken into account.

The importance of the kenosis motif as a basic theme of New Testament thought was first underlined by certain theologians and Bible scholars of the last century. Gottfried Thomasius, August Ebrard, H. R. Mackintosh, and others who championed the kenotic Christologies of their time saw the possibilities for finding the kenosis motif in the New Testament as almost limitless. Attempting to find Biblical backing for their position, they perceived that the whole New Testament can be arranged into a proof text for the kenotic Christology. It is simply necessary to place in juxtaposition the many references to Christ's preexistent glory as a sharer in the divine life and all the references to his humiliation, limitations, suffering, and death in the earthly ministry. Then it can be argued that the only way in which these two opposite states of existence could be predicated of the same person is by some process of divine self-limitation. Arguing on these grounds, the kenosis motif does not so much represent one type of Christological thought in the New Testament as a principle by which to interpret all Christological thought. H. R. Mackintosh, who took this position, said, "The kenotic theory is put forward to synthesize the facts definitely before us." [3] For him these "facts" were the preexistent life of Christ sharing the glory of the Trinity and his fully human life as Jesus of Nazareth. In this approach to the New Testament, the kenotic conception of Christology is not simply one theory among many; it is the one and final theory of Christology in all New Testament thought.

As valuable as this approach is for understanding the basic importance of the kenosis motif, it really sought to prove too much. For while it is clear that the kenotic motif is one of the ways in which the earliest Christians related the preexistent and the earthly life of Christ, it was not their only interpretation of Christ. The existence of other approaches to this question in the New Testament is too evident to be denied. The scholarship of the nineteenth century was right in pointing out the importance of all that the New Testament says about the preexistent life of Christ and his earthly life of full humanity as a necessary background to the kenosis motif. Without this, the idea of a divine self-emptying in Christ would be unintelligible. But this contrast between the heavenly and earthly existence of Christ does not of itself prove the universal validity of the kenotic theory.

To bring into clear focus what the New Testament says about kenosis, it is necessary to proceed from the background of all that is said about the preexistent and the earthly life of Christ to the specific kenotic formulas. In the specifically kenotic passages the general motif is given concrete formulation. The *locus classicus* of the kenotic motif is clearly Phil. 2:5-11. Ranged along with this are such passages as II Cor. 8:9; John 3:13; 16:28; 17:5; and Rom. 15:3. In the history of exegesis the focus of attention has always been the Philippian passage because it is the most detailed. The other passages were generally read in the light of deductions made on the basis of the fuller presentation in Philippians. This approach commends itself, allowing us to proceed from the less obscure to the more obscure. After critical examination of the Philippians passage, the rest of the New Testament evidence can be put into perspective.

In approaching the exegesis of Phil. 2:5-11, we must take note of the heavy hand of tradition on our thought. For to a unique degree the understanding of this passage has been dominated by the patterns of thought established in the anti-Arian controversy of the fourth century and perpetuated uncritically until almost our own time. In order to transcend this particular exegesis, it is necessary first to understand it. For the whole modern attempt to read the Philippian passage in its own terms represents a struggle with the traditional exegesis that was so heavily impressed upon the mind of the church in those early centuries. Before we can go beyond the traditional exegesis, we must take a serious look at it.

The Traditional Exegesis of Phil. 2:5-11

The traditional exegesis of Phil. 2:5-11 was the work of the anti-Arian fathers. The Arians, it seems, seized on the ambiguity of the term " in the form of God " (ch. 2:6) as a means of promulgating their doctrine that Christ was of a created or only semidivine nature. He was not fully God, they argued, but was " in the form of God." The Christ was a creature, albeit the first and highest, but he was not a fully divine, eternal member of the Godhead as the orthodox maintained. To answer this argument, the orthodox exegetes, Victorinus (d. ca.

304) and Athanasius (ca. 296–373), undertook the clarification of the terms " in the form of God " (ch. 2:6) and " he emptied himself" (ch. 2:7). Their determinations on these points dominated the main line of exegesis from the fathers through all the Catholic exegetes to Calvin and Reformed orthodoxy down to the nineteenth century. Their point was very simple. To be " in the form of God " does not imply any subordination to God as the Arians held. Rather, it means to be fully equal and coeternal with God the Father. To say that the Christ is " in the form of God " is another way of saying that he is the Second Person of the Trinity. All thoughts of a lesser or created nature for Christ that may be implied by the term " in the form of God " were rejected. On this basis the passage was construed to say: " The Christ who was fully divine did not count equality with God a thing to be grasped (because he already possessed it) but freely emptied himself to enter the human realm of suffering and death. God then exalted him, revealing his true nature in returning him to the glory of the Godhead and calling all creation to worship him." The three key phrases used to characterize the divine status of Christ — " in the form of God " (ch. 2:6), " equal with God " (ch. 2:6), and the name of " Lord " (ch. 2:11) — were read as exact equivalents. The self-emptying of Christ and his consequent exaltation did not represent any real change in his fully divine nature. The status of the Christ as the Second Person of the Trinity was by its very nature unchangeable.

The kenosis implied in ch. 2:7, " he emptied himself," was taken to mean a veiling or obscuring of the divine glory during the earthly ministry of Jesus. This was usually referred to as the divine occultation, *occultatio Dei.* In this conception the kenosis did not imply a lessening of the divine nature. It implied simply its covering or obscuring during Jesus' earthly ministry. Kenosis was the assumption by the Second Person of the Trinity of a veil of human flesh by which incarnation was possible. This kenosis was willed by Christ himself as the means by which he could carry out his ministry of suffering and death.

As Calvin later explained it, " for a time the divine glory did not shine, but only human likeness was manifest in a lowly and abased condition." [4] The assumption of flesh does not imply a lessening of the divine nature. This is made clear when the earthly ministry is finished and Christ is exalted by the Father. Then the true nature of Christ is revealed in resurrection and ascension. The veil of flesh is transformed by the divine glory, and all men are made to know Christ for who he really is: the Lord of all.

The factors that went into the modern criticism and restatement of this exegesis of the Philippian passage are many and complex. They will become clearer as the history of the kenosis motif unfolds. But two crucial weaknesses in the traditional exegesis can be seen right now. First, it is not clear that the term " in the form of God " means full equality or identity with God. Indeed, at this point the Arians are closer to the obvious meaning of the term. To be " in the form of God " implies similarity to God, not identity. " In the form of God " is construed most naturally in a manner similar to the phrase " in the image of God." To say that man is " in the image of God " implies a similarity to God but certainly not full equality. In the same way, to be " in the form of God " implies that Christ has a high degree of similarity to God, but not full identity. To make their point against the Arians, orthodoxy gave the phrase a meaning it does not have when taken in its most obvious linguistic sense. Second, the veiling or occultation of the divine nature of Christ during his earthly ministry is not the same as an emptying of that nature. Occultation implies a hiding, not a loss or diminution of the divine nature. To interpret " he emptied himself " as the hiding of the divine glory behind a veil of flesh bespeaks a docetism that is foreign to the clear meaning of the text. The divine mode of existence had been relinquished, not simply hidden from view. Yet these obvious objections to the traditional exegesis were never made until modern times. It was only as the church struggled with new philosophical and theological thought that it was enabled to approach the kenotic passages afresh. This fresh approach revolutionized patterns of thought that had been set for over fifteen hundred years.

The criticism and restatement of the traditional exegesis of the Philippian passage got its start in the nineteenth century. But full critico-historical study of the kenosis motif itself is actually the work of the present century. The restudy of the vital Philippian passage has followed three approaches: an analysis of the literary style, a detailed study of the key words by the techniques of comparative philology, and a search for the mythopoetic background of the kenosis motif in contemporary Jewish and Hellenistic literature. From these modern studies of the Philippian passage certain major features of the kenosis motif have emerged with clarity. Yet much remains in the area of uncertainty and conflict. For to a unique degree the study of the kenosis motif moves in an area where scientific, historical method and theological commitment mesh inextricably. Hence the yeas are never finally yeas, nor the nays, nays.

The Literary Form of the Philippian Passage

The first key in unlocking the meaning of Phil. 2:5-11 is the determination of its literary style. The literary form of the passage is an important key to the questions of authorship, origins, and the use of words within it. It is important to determine whether the passage reflects the subtle distinctions of language that befit formal theological discourse or whether, like a hymn or liturgy, it is essentially poetic in nature. Analysis of the style and form can also reveal whether the passage is a literary whole or is a fragmentary quotation.

The importance of such questions was first appreciated by Johannes Weiss and Adolf Deissmann, who questioned the Pauline authorship of these verses. They raised the possibility that these verses were an earlier hymn that Paul quoted to support his admonition to humility to the Philippian congregation. Modern exegesis pondered the question of style and its significance for interpretation with the growing conviction that the passage is a separate hymn characterized by a unique vocabulary and metrical structure. The main consideration that pointed to a separate authorship for the Philippian passage was the way it related to the rest of the epistle. As a whole Philippians is written freely, with little regard for the well-turned rhetorical phrase. In the midst of this informality, the lofty style and balanced structure of ch. 2:6-11 stands out clearly. Exegetes have been aware of this shift for some time. It was generally assumed that Paul had modified his style to meet the loftiness of the theme he was treating. Paul starts his admonition to humility in ch. 2:5 with the introductory phrase: " Have this mind among yourselves, which you have in Christ Jesus." Then he goes on to describe the " mind " or " spirit " that is given in Christ. If this introductory phrase is separated from what follows, the material in vs. 6-11 reflects a formal structure that seems to be derived from the rythmic pattern of a hymn.

Ernst Lohmeyer has given the most detailed analysis of the structure of vs. 6-11.[5] It contains two stanzas: vs. 6-8, which tell of the divine self-emptying and life of humiliation and death, and vs. 9-11, which tell of the resultant glorification and worship. Each stanza is made of three verses of three lines each. The two stanzas are analogous. They form a literary unit. For not only is the structure balanced, but so is the content. The movement of thought is from eternity back to eternity. The hymn starts with him who is of the divine realm. It tells of his coming to earth, and it ends with his return to the divine realm, where he is worshiped. Both the form and the contents reflect the rules of parallelism found in the Hebrew religious verse of the Old Testament.

Such a literary analysis commends itself in general outline, although close scrutiny reveals that the text does not really conform to Lohmeyer's pattern. The first stanza, for example, contains ten lines instead of the requisite nine. The all-important phrase " even the death of the cross " (v. 8) is outside the structure. In contrast to Lohmeyer's minute analysis, Joachim Jeremias has suggested a less detailed structure that would con-

THE TEXT OF PHIL. 2:5-11 ARRANGED IN METRICAL
ORDER ACCORDING TO THE SUGGESTIONS OF
LOHMEYER AND JEREMIAS

Have this mind among yourselves, which you have
in Christ Jesus,

Lohmeyer's *Analysis*	*First Stanza*	*Jeremias'* *Analysis*
STROPHE I	Who being in the form of God did not count it something to be grasped to be equal with God,	STANZA 1
STROPHE II	but emptied himself, taking the form of a servant, being born in the likeness of men.	
STROPHE III	And being found in human fashion, he humbled himself and became obedient unto death (even death on a cross).	STANZA 2

Second Stanza

STROPHE IV	Therefore God has highly exalted him and bestowed on him the name which is above all names,	
STROPHE V	that at the name of Jesus every knee should bow in heaven and on earth and under the earth,	STANZA 3
STROPHE VI	and every tongue confess that Jesus Christ is Lord to the glory of God the Father.	

form more fully to the actual content of the hymn. He divides
it into three stanzas: vs. 6-7b, 7-8, and 9-11. This has the ad-
vantage of setting forth the threefold modes of existence of
Christ. The first stanza concerns the preexistent Christ; the
second stanza sets forth the life of humiliation and death; the
last stanza tells of the glorification. A more minute analysis of
the structure is not really possible.

It is clear that this passage is a hymn. But it was not composed as a paradigm of classical style. Its parallelism is only of a very general sort. It was probably a hymn that grew out of the earliest Christian worship. Although it shows affinities to the classical Hebrew forms, it should not be read wholly in that light. In any case, the important fact for exegesis is the recognition of Phil. 2:6-11 as a separate literary unit of poetical structure.

The deductions made on the basis of literary style and vocabulary concerning the authorship of the hymn have been of three kinds:

1. There are those who hold that Paul wrote the hymn himself to lift before the Philippians the supreme example of humility eloquently expressed. In this way his point could be more persuasively presented. The general line of thought in the hymn is clearly compatible with Pauline Christology. The hymn is echoed again in II Cor. 8:9. But it seems labored to assume that in the midst of an intensely practical epistle of informal style Paul would compose a special hymn. The evidence points in another direction.

2. Ernst Barnikol has argued from the literary form and doctrine of the hymn that it was a second-century Marcionite-Gnostic fragment inserted in the text of the epistle to gain apostolic sanction for it.[6] But such a thesis overlooks the anti-Gnostic tone of the hymn that stresses the reality of Jesus' human life and the ignominy of his death. " He became obedient unto death, even the death of the cross." (Phil. 2:8.)

3. Actually the place of the hymn in the epistle points in a direction opposite to that taken by Barnikol in dating it. It is rather, as Lohmeyer has suggested, an indication that this hymn is pre-Pauline in origin. It was an established piece of tradition to which Paul made reference as clinching evidence in his admonition to the Philippian Christians. The very force of the hymn at this point in the epistle is that it was a commonly shared piece of tradition linking Paul and his readers. It is a primitive liturgical form culminating in the confessional state-

ment, " Jesus Christ is Lord " (ch. 2:11). As such, it points back to the early unfolding of the mind of the church about its Lord.

" The Form of God "

The considerations of literary style have opened afresh the study of the key words in the hymn. The key phrases in the exegesis of the hymn are: " in the form of God," " the form of a servant," and " he emptied himself." The verb *kenoō*, which characterizes the all-important transition in v. 7 — " he emptied himself " — from the divine to the earthly realm of existence, has no particular philosophical use in Greek. It means simply " to empty," or it can mean " to make void, of no effect." " He emptied himself " is a graphic metaphor expressing the completeness of Christ's self-renunciation. The varied interpretations of what constituted divine self-emptying cannot find any support in a detailed study of the meaning of the verb. But such is not the case with the all-important word *morphē* in the phrases " in the form of God " and " form of a servant."

Morphē has a long and involved history of uses in Greek philosophical and religious literature. During the nineteenth century, Bishop Lightfoot and others tried to find a linguistic basis for the traditional exegesis of the hymn.[7] They interpreted *morphē* in the light of parallels in classical Greek. *Morphē* was taken as equivalent to *eidos* or " idea " as found in Plato. " Form " was another word to characterize the eternal ideas or archetypes that make up ultimate reality. Hence, to be " in the form " of something was to participate fully in ultimate reality and to share its eternal quality. To say that Christ was " in the form of God " means he shares fully in the nature of God. He is consubstantial and coeternal with God. But this line of argument is anachronistic. For this first-century liturgical hymn is far removed from the subtle distinctions of thought found in the philosophy of Plato and Aristotle. Its use of words is not that of exact philosophical discourse. The hymn uses the religious language of liturgy and confession. Its parallels are to be found rather in contemporary religious literature, particularly that of later Jewish and Hellenistic times.

Modern lexical studies, particularly those of Johannes Behm, have shown that *morphē* had a variety of inexact meanings in Hellenistic Greek.[8] In refuting the Arians the orthodox exegetes had imposed a clarity on the term that it did not really possess. " In the form " did not imply full identity or equality of essence. In Hellenistic religious and philosophical literature the " form " sometimes indicates an archetype or eternal image; at other times it means simply the outward appearance. In places it refers to inner reality or being; in others, merely to shape. The distinction between these two possible meanings is determined by the context in which the word is found.

In the Philippian hymn the reference is to the inner reality of Christ's person. It describes his relation to God in terms of sharing in the divine nature. The use of *morphē* here signifies a form that truly expresses the being which underlies it and participates in its life. Although there is not full identity, there is continuity between the " form " and its underlying reality. The " form " does not belie the underlying reality it expresses. Hence, the Christ truly expresses the divine reality. But he is not identical with God.

The Mythological Setting of the Kenosis Motif

The literary and philological analysis of the Philippian hymn taken by itself does not yield enough evidence for a full exegesis. To complete the exegesis it is necessary to discover the immediate background of religious thought from which the hymn emerged. This background has been reconstructed in extensive studies by Otto Dibelius, Oscar Cullmann, and Ernst Käsemann of the literature of the late Jewish and Hellenistic period.[9] The study of the rabbinic and apocalyptic literature of Judaism and that of Hellenistic Gnosticism have shown illuminating parallels to the New Testament kenosis motif, and have also helped to clarify the meaning of the all-important phrase " in the form of God."

There is in both Jewish and Hellenistic religious literature of the New Testament period a belief in the existence of heavenly beings in the realm of the divine who share the glory of God. One of the most commonly encountered figures in these Jewish and Hellenistic religious speculations is that of the Heavenly or Primal Man. This figure is known by a number of titles. He is sometimes called the Son of Man, or sometimes Adam. He is the Original or Archetypal Man who exists in the perfect image or form of God. This Heavenly Man is the perfect image of God in human form. The Archetypal Man has even in his preexistence in the heavenly realm a human form. In the first tractate of the *Hermetica*, a collection of Gnostic myths from the first century, there is an account of how a Heavenly Man came onto the plane of historical existence. Mind, the Father of all, generated a Man who possessed the "form of God," entered the realm of nature — or empirical human existence — and "inhabited the irrational form." After existing for some time in this form, he was able to reenter the heavenly realm. This return to the heavenly realm was the means of saving men who could share in his victory over the irrational forces that hold humanity in bondage. In this myth the Heavenly Man becomes the Redeemer. He moves from sharing in the divine realm to the realm of ordinary human life and then returns. In doing this, he brings about the redemption of mankind.

The picture of the Heavenly Man who preexists with God is also found in rabbinic exegesis of the Creation stories of Genesis and in Jewish apocalyptic writings of the New Testament period. The emphasis is different here than in the Hermetic literature. The Heavenly Man is frequently identified as Adam failed in his responsibility to express his true nature as the of God. But he did not remain loyal to his destiny as the perfect creature of God. Rather, he falsely aspired after equality with God. Because of this Satanic grasping after God, he fell from his place in the divine realm where he shared the glory of God. By contrast with the grasping of Adam, in the Philippian hymn,

Christ is pictured as fulfilling his destiny as the true Heavenly Man by accepting the humble " form of a servant." This seems to be the contrast suggested in Phil. 2:6: " He did not count equality with God a thing to be grasped." A similar contrast is also drawn in other New Testament passages where Christ is contrasted with Adam: Rom. 5:12 ff. and I Cor. 15:45 ff. Adam failed in his responsibility to express his true nature as the " image " or " form of God." Christ fulfilled his true nature as the Heavenly Man who preexisted in the " form of God " because he accepted the suffering and death of a servant.

Although there are many variations on this theme of a pre-existent Heavenly Man in the literature of the time, certain features do appear clearly. (1) The Heavenly Man is a being in the " form " or " image " of God. He is a creature of God who, while subordinate to God, still shares the divine being. During his preexistence in the heavenly realm he lives in the presence of the divine glory. But this does not imply that he is a full member of the Godhead. Even in his preexistence the One " in the form of God " is already a man. He is usually pictured as an Archetypal Man rather than a particular historical man. He does not take on the character of a particular, empirical human person until he enters the realm of earthly existence. Yet it remains clear that his being during his preexistence is both human and divine. (2) This being " in the form of God " is able to determine his own destiny. He could choose the destructive course of grasping after " equality with God " or he could " empty himself, taking the form of a servant." Hence, the action of the Heavenly Man can become the source of a moral appeal.

The Message of the Philippian Hymn

What do these modern approaches to the form and content of the hymn tell us of its message? This can best be seen by viewing the passage in broad outline and then seeing how the details can be elaborated. The hymn presents a picture of the redemption wrought by Christ that is simple in outline: a semidivine being leaves the heavenly realm freely to enter the realm of human life with its suffering and death (Phil. 2:6-8). Because of his life of obedience and suffering, ending in ignominious death, he is glorified and given a new status or name — that of "Lord" — which allows him to be worshiped by all creation. (Ch. 2:9-11.) This semidivine being was the Christ who is none other than Jesus who had lived and died and has risen.

What is the status of this Christ in his preexistence in the divine realm? Its exact character is indeterminate. Too great clarity or exactness would belie the evidence. He exists "in the form of God," which means he is of the divine order. The relation of the preincarnate Christ to God was genuine and real. He shared in what is characteristic of God. But at the same time he is the preexistent Heavenly Man, the pure image of God who is a God-man already in his preexistence. Although he shares in the divine life, he is not fully equal to God in this preincarnate state. Some of the modern paraphrases of "in the form of God" are helpful in grasping its meaning without the controversy-laden language of the traditional translation. Moffatt suggests "he was divine by nature." C. Masson uses "divine condition" to render the phrase. These may lack the vividness of "in the form of God," but they do convey the idea of a real relation without an implied identity. The identification of the preexistent Christ with God as the unchangeable Second Person of the Trinity reflects a much later development of doctrine. This later development cannot be read back into this early strand of tradition.

The Christ having been described as a preexistent divine-human being, the Heavenly Man, the contrast is now drawn between him and Adam who was also in the form or image of God. Unlike Adam, the Christ "did not count equality with God a thing to be grasped." He freely accepted entrance into the human realm of sin and death. The actual transition of the Heavenly Man into the realm of empirical humanity is characterized by the phrase "he emptied himself." The immediate subject of the verb is the preexistent Christ. Just what was emptied is not made clear. The inner meaning of the phrase remains mute to speculative probings. The suggestion that he emptied himself of certain divine attributes while leaving the essence of his divinity untouched is a form of anachronistic reasoning from presuppositions foreign to the New Testament. Perhaps it was his glory, as suggested later in John 17:5. This much is clear from the context: the emptying was an act of obedient sacrifice in which the freedom of the divine realm from the power of sin and death is put aside for the bondage of human life to these powers. The emptying was the assumption of sinful humanity for its redemption. This is the significance of kenosis given in II Cor. 8:9. " For you know the grace of our Lord Jesus Christ, that though he was rich, yet for your sake he became poor, so that by his poverty you might become rich." This exchange was possible only because the Christ had emptied or impoverished himself by forswearing the divine freedom for the bondage of fallen humanity.

Verses 7b-8 describe the earthly life of the Christ. In distinction to the " form of God," the Christ now dwells " in the form of a slave." He was born " in the likeness of men " and " found in human form." In this form he perfected his obedience through humbly accepting " death, even the death of the cross." It is in this act of obedience that the contrast to Adam is complete. In this act of obedience Christ accepts the role of the Suffering Servant. The Second Adam, who is the Suffering Servant, overcomes the first Adam's sin of disobedience. In contrast to all human attempts at self-salvation through self-assertion, the Christ brings salvation through self-abasement.

Verses 9-11 deal with the exaltation of Christ that follows his earthly ministry. The section is opened by the conjunction *dio*, which is usually translated " therefore " or " in consequence of which." It indicates a resultant or causal relation with what went before. Because of his self-emptying and humility, God has " exalted him in superlative measure " (v. 9), and " graciously bestowed upon him that name which is above every name." The exaltation of Christ in the resurrection-ascension was earned by his humble obedience. It resulted in a real change of status. The Christ who was "in the form of God" was given something that he did not previously possess — " the name which is above every name," i.e., the name of "Lord." Because of this exaltation, the Christ is now an object of worship. The One who had humbled himself to the point of death on a cross was now to be worshiped by all. His dominion is complete over all things "in heaven and on earth and under the earth." All knees shall bow before him, and all will confess his new status as Lord. This is indicated in the confessional statement of v. 11: "Jesus Christ is Lord, to the glory of God the Father."

The relation of the exalted Christ to God is closer than that which he had had in his preexistence. The One who was "in the form of God" was subordinate to God and not the object of worship. The exalted Christ is now the Lord worshiped by all. The use of the term "Lord" or *Kyrios*, as the new title for Christ, is of crucial importance here. *Kyrios* is the Greek translation of the divine name "Yahweh." *Kyrios* is used in the Septuagint as the name of God the Father. The use of this term as the name of the exalted Christ indicated that there had been bestowed on him the name and power of God himself. This was a status he did not have in his preexistence or during his earthly ministry. The significance of the giving of this title had been overlooked by traditional exegesis. Traditional exegesis equated the preexistent and the exalted states. Since Christ had always been fully equal with God, no new status could be given him. The exaltation was taken to mean the revelation of Christ's true divine status, which had been obscured during the earthly ministry. There is pictured in the text, rather, a dynamic movement within the divine life itself. The Christ had entered a new and exalted plane of being in which he stood on a level with God himself.

The Philippian hymn represents a stage of doctrinal development similar to that found in Hebrews, particularly the prologue, Heb. 1:4. In this passage the Son, who was preexistent, received a higher status or name because of his earthly ministry. Similarly, in Heb. 2:9, Jesus is said to be " crowned with glory and honor" because he had suffered death. The Christ was made perfect or complete through his sufferings. (Heb. 2:10 and 5:9.) In these passages there is an attempt to reconcile the adoptionism of the earlier Christologies — indications of which are found in the early sermons of The Acts and in the Gospels — to the growing belief in the preexistence of Christ. The uniquely stressed element of exaltation to a new status associated with the resurrection-ascension in the earlier adoptionist traditions is retained. In his exaltation Christ is given a new and higher status that he did not have before. He received this status because he had been faithful in his mission of suffering and death. In Philippians and in Hebrews this earlier tradition of adoptionism is combined with the emerging belief in the preexistence of Christ. However, his preexistent life is on a lower level or status than that which he entered in his exaltation. Although Christ preexisted in the divine realm, he did not hold the status of Lord until he completed a life of faithful obedience and suffering. In this way there was real point to believing in an exaltation of Christ even while holding belief in his preexistence. Subsequent developments in Christology in the New Testament and early church moved beyond the position of Philippians and Hebrews toward equating the status of the preexistent and exalted Christ. This is seen already in the Fourth Gospel. Such a development meant that the unique element of elevation to a new status for Christ at his resurrection-ascension was lost. The exaltation becomes simply the return to the glories of the Godhead in which Christ had always participated fully. But in the Philippian hymn itself the element of exaltation to a new status still had an important part.

The Kenosis Motif in the New Testament as a Whole

The setting of the explicitly kenotic passage of II Cor. 8:9, like that in Philippians, is a practical admonition. The Co-

rinthians are being encouraged to liberality in the collection for
the needy of the Jerusalem church. Again as in Philippians, the
example of Christ is held before his readers by Paul. "For you
know the grace of our Lord Jesus Christ, that though he was
rich, yet for your sake he became poor, so that by his poverty
you might become rich." In keeping with the purpose of the
passage, the contrast between richness and poverty is used to
picture the self-emptying act of Christ. The picture is less detailed than in Philippians. The exact meaning of richness and
poverty is left undefined. But the contrast is clear. There is,
on the one hand, the richness and creativity of the divine realm
in which Christ preexisted and to which he returns mankind.
In contrast to this, there is the poverty of human existence, the
realm of sin and death, which Christ freely accepted in order
to deliver man to the richness of life in the divine realm. The
source and ultimate explanation of this free saving act of renunciation was the "grace of our Lord Jesus Christ." Here, as
in Philippians, the most characteristic act of the gracious God
is not assertion but abnegation.

The Fourth Gospel contains all the elements of the kenosis
motif, although they are not brought fully into relation to one
another. From the prologue onward there are the repeated assertions of Christ's preexistence with the Father. He is the
Word of God who is one with the Father. (John 1:1; 10:30;
14:10; etc.) The Word became flesh and took up a life that
was genuinely human. In entering human life, Christ has forsaken the glory that he had with the Father from all eternity.
(Ch. 17:5 and v. 24.) This is precisely the glory which he will
again assume in his glorification, that is, in his resurrection-
ascension. "Father, glorify thou me in thy own presence with
the glory which I had with thee before the world was made."
(Ch. 17:5.)

In the Fourth Gospel there is a paradoxical element to the
conception of the divine kenosis. The glory the Son receives
from the Father is not completely absent during the earthly
ministry. John 1:14 makes it clear that even in the Word made

flesh " we have beheld his glory, glory as of the only Son from the Father." The earthly life involves a limitation of the divine glory. Yet this does not mean an extinction of the divine glory or mode of existence. There is a revelation of the divine glory in the human figure of Jesus, his work and destiny.

The Fourth Gospel does not elaborate on the kenosis motif. The exact nature or extent of the kenosis is not given. The same general outline obtains here as in the Philippian hymn. But now the Christ is pictured as sharing fully the divine life in his preexistence. He empties himself to take up a human life. But in this life some of the glory he had in his preexistence is still present. When his earthly ministry is finished, he returns to the glory that had been his before in the presence of his Father. Glorification is not an exaltation to a new status; it is now simply the return to a divine status that was unchangeable by its very nature.

This chapter started with the assertion that viewed in a particular way the possibilities of finding evidence of the kenosis motif in the New Testament are almost limitless. The procedure was to arrange in juxtaposition the references to Christ's preexistent glory and those to his earthly life of limitation, suffering, and death. Then it could be argued that the only way in which these two states can be predicated of the same person is on the basis of some form of kenosis. This method was put aside in favor of studying only those places in which the motif is explicitly drawn. Yet this more discursive approach used by many of the nineteenth-century scholars of the kenotic motif gives an important perspective in evaluating its importance for the New Testament as a whole. So, having analyzed in detail the specific kenotic formulas, one finds it possible to appraise their importance for the whole New Testament.

The basic importance of the kenosis motif is that it provides a means for integrating and interpreting the whole of the New Testament witness to Jesus Christ in all its richness. This was the understanding of the kenosis motif of men such as Thomasius, Gore, and Mackintosh. They recognized that if the kenosis motif were only a matter of thus and so many specific references in the New Testament, it would rate but a small niche in the structure of Christian thought. The importance of the kenosis motif is found, rather, in the way it shapes and informs the various approaches to the meaning of Christ. Its significance in New Testament thought is precisely because it is a broad motif. And as the word "motif" implies, it is a recurrent, integrating theme in which the meaning of the whole is comprehended. The motif of the divine self-emptying is an inevitable outgrowth of the full Christian faith in Jesus Christ. It is a motif that arises immediately out of the experience of new life in Christ that the earliest Christians had.

It was clear to the faith of the early church that in Christ they were encountering the one, holy God. In him they met the God who had thundered at Sinai, the One who had spoken by the prophets, the One whose action in judgment and redemption had marked out the course of their history as the people of God. "In many and various ways God spoke of old to our fathers by the prophets; but in these last days he has spoken to us by a Son." (Heb. 1:1-2a.) In Jesus Christ they knew that God met them in a startlingly new way. Now God encountered them in a human life beset with the limitations, sufferings, and finally death to which every man is heir. They believed God had stood where each one of us stands amidst the frailties of human life. They believed that God had accepted this limitation. God had accepted the limitations of a human life and yet had not ceased being God. It was a self-limitation, a kenosis by which human salvation was accomplished. This is a faith common to the whole of the New Testament. This is not a fully formulated kenotic doctrine in the modern sense. It is rather a broad motif of faith that lies behind the New Testament picture of Jesus Christ. It is in this sense that the whole of the New Testament gives evidence of the kenotic motif.

CHAPTER III

The Struggle with the Hellenistic Spirit

THE KENOSIS MOTIF IN THE PATRISTIC AGE AND THE MEDIEVAL CHURCH

The Meaning of Hellenization

From the first century to the fifth century the thought and life of the church underwent changes that dominated it until modern times. The impress of this age is still seen in the doctrinal formulas, the theological language, and the institutional forms of Christianity. Christian faith was no longer to be expressed simply in the language and thought forms of late Judaism. As the Christian faith left the narrow confines of its first-century beginnings for the wider world of Greco-Roman antiquity, its faith was spoken in new and strange languages. It encountered the spirit and mind of Greco-Roman antiquity. And out of this encounter was fashioned the doctrinal formulas that were destined to define Christian orthodoxy to this day. The doctrines of the Trinity and the two natures of Christ were defined in this period. These doctrines have set the tone for Christological discussion ever since. During this period a pattern of thought was also set that determined fully the place of the kenosis motif for almost fifteen hundred years. The history of the motif during the patristic age highlights to a remarkable degree the inner development of doctrine in that crucial period. Its reformulation demonstrates the radical reorientation of Christianity through its encounter with the mind and spirit of Greco-Roman antiquity.

In the approach to the historical development of an idea in Christian thought during the patristic period, it is wise to make clear certain presuppositions one inevitably carries into the study. Since the issues at stake in this period are so momentus — the proper understanding of God, of Christ, and of salvation — partisan arguments have waxed hot over just how Christianity was transformed. The Christian faith by the end of the patristic age was no longer expressed through the language and thought forms of late Judaism, but rather those of the Greco-Roman world. To see this, one need only read the New Testament and compare it with the Canons of Chalcedon, the Creed of Nicaea, or the theology of Athanasius. That there was this basic change in the modes of expressing the faith no one could deny. To use Adolf Harnack's phrase, there had been a " Hellenization of the gospel." But this is not the important issue at stake. The real question is just how this Hellenization affected the Christian faith itself. In this change called Hellenization was the inner quality of the Christian faith, the quality by which it is called gospel — good news — lost, or was it merely reexpressed? Had the gospel been enhanced by fresh expression or had it been lost?

Until the advent of modern historical science in the eighteenth century, Christians had assumed that doctrine underwent no real change. Christians believed, in the words of the Vincentian canon, their faith was that which was believed " everywhere, at all times, by everyone" in the church. The doctrine of the church was true, and since truth is changeless, doctrine is changeless. To the degree to which they traced the growth of doctrine through the ages, they understood it simply as a translation. The doctrines of the New Testament were simply and exactly translated into the theology and creeds of the patristic age. They believed that by proper exegesis, frequently allegorical in method, Scripture would validate church doctrine fully. They believed there was a simple, direct continuity between the preaching of Jesus and his disciples and the creeds and canons of the church. The language may have changed from Aramaic and Greek to Latin, but the substance of thought and faith was unchanged.

With the advent of modern historical study, a new thesis gained currency. The claim was made that this Hellenization was not simply a matter of translation without change of inner substance. Historians recognized that Hellenism was a spiritual and intellectual force from outside Christianity. And as Christianity encountered the Hellenistic spirit, it was transformed into something alien to that of its Founder. The change from the Christianity of the New Testament to that of the fifth century was not a simple growth. There was a radical break between the two in which the unique moral and spiritual values of primitive Christianity had been lost. In place of the gospel had come a doctrinal structure and hierarchical church that expressed the Greco-Roman mind far more than the mind of Christ. Hellenization was in large part the triumph of an alien spirit over original Christianity. Much popular historical scholarship has championed this position. Certainly there has been much in the work of the great historians of nineteenth-century Germany to support such a view, although it must be added in all fairness that good historians never put the matter in as oversimplified form as has been done here.

The important insight of these modern historians of doctrine is that Hellenism is a spiritual and intellectual force in itself that affected the core of the faith. Hellenistic antiquity reshaped not only the language but also the mind and spirit of Christianity. But it is incorrect to assume thereby that Hellenism was a Procrustean bed that foreshortened Christianity to its own peculiar dimensions. As Charles N. Cochrane demonstrated in *Christianity and Classical Culture*, the very substance of Hellenism was changed by Christianity. The relation between Christianity and the culture of Greco-Roman antiquity was not simply a one-way street in either direction. There is, rather, a complex interaction between the two. This interaction can best be described by the analogy of human conversation or dialogue. If there is real dialogue, both parties seek to understand one another. They must speak one another's language. The inevitable result, however, is that in this conversation both parties are themselves changed. The Hellenization of the gospel was the conversation between the church and the Greco-Roman world. It was a conversation to which the church was impelled by its missionary zeal. It was a conversation that the church could not have avoided if it was to survive. It was a conversation in which the church learned to speak a new language and in so doing took on new forms of life. The Christianity that emerged at the end of the patristic age was not a mere restatement of the New Testament faith. It was a religion that had knit into its fabric intellectual and organizational patterns that lay far beyond the scope of the most primitive church. By some of these patterns of life the gospel was enhanced, by others it was denied. In no place is this made clearer than in the changes and reinterpretations of the kenosis motif by the fathers.

To gauge the changes in interpretation of kenosis during the patristic age, it is necessary to summarize the ideas associated with this motif in the New Testament. There were four basic assertions of Christian faith related by the kenosis: (1) Belief in the preexistence of Christ. Christ had shared in the richness of the divine life and had existed " in the form of God." (II Cor. 8:9; Phil. 2:6; John 1:1; Heb. 1:2-3; etc.) (2) Belief in the reality of his human life as Jesus of Nazareth. Christ had shared the poverty of human life in the " form of a servant," finally sharing in death. (II Cor. 8:9; Phil. 2:7-9; I John 4:2; etc.) (3) Belief in the exaltation of Christ to the status of Lord in his resurrection-ascension. (II Cor. 8:9; Phil. 2:9-11; Matt. 28:18; etc.) (4) Belief in the redemption that was accomplished by Christ through his ministry of self-emptying love. The Christ had become poor that through him men could share the riches of God. The believers could now share the glory that Christ had with his Father before the foundation of the earth. (II Cor. 8:9; John 17:24; Phil. 2:10; etc.) The divine self-emptying was the key that set this whole drama of salvation into motion.

Each one of these four beliefs associated with the kenotic motif underwent major change through the work of the fathers that culminated in the statements of Nicaea and Chalcedon. The doctrine of the preexistence and the exaltation of Christ were coordinated into one by the Trinitarian formula. The Christ was declared to be the Second Person of the Trinity, coequal and coeternal with the Father. Christ's being was eternal and unchangeable. So any notion of exaltation to a new and higher status was ruled out. Christ's status was the same before and after his earthly ministry. The nature of Christ's person during his earthly ministry was restated in the doctrine of the two natures. He was described as fully human and fully divine. The humanity simply clothed or veiled the deity. The note of full identity with men as a man was lost. The redemption given through Christ was now described as his power to give immortality to men through the deification of their flesh. The notion of the imminent coming of salvation at the end of history in an event embracing all mankind was replaced by the idea of personal salvation. Christ was Savior by virtue of his power to make men immortal.

The factors that brought about these changes are numerous and complex. These reformulations absorbed the mind of the church for over three centuries. Any generalizations about such a long and complex change in the basic patterns of Christian thought are difficult to make. Yet in connection with the kenotic motif certain features are clear. As the kenotic motif is found in the New Testament it is expressed through mythological thought forms. The conception of God is intensely personalistic and dynamic. The patristic restatement of the motif was dominated by philosophical thought forms in which the conception of God was fundamentally abstract and static.

Biblical thought is dominated by a highly personal conception of God. The way in which the Bible abounds in anthropomorphisms gives abundant testimony to this. God loves and hates. He feels sorrow and joy. He is moved to compassion and to anger. God is not thought of abstractly as the source of being. He is a person who encounters us in judgment and redemption. The self-emptying of God is his free personal act. It is not determined by some abstract metaphysical necessity. Rather, it is grounded in the fact that God wishes to encounter men as a man. The kenosis springs from the free act of Christ. " He did not count equality with God a thing to be grasped." (Phil. 2:6.) Paul could point to Christ's kenosis as an example of humility and generosity because Christ had freely accepted self-emptying for the sake of others. Kenosis is the free, personal act of God.

Closely coordinated with the personalism of New Testament thought is its acceptance of dynamic modes of thought in describing the nature of God. God is free to act in any and all ways. He is free to change and to accept different means of self-expression. In the Old Testament God is pictured as sorrowing for his people in their bondage. He grows angry with their sins. Then he repents of his anger. Finally, in the New Testament God is revealed as sharing in suffering and death through Jesus Christ. God takes into his person the forces of suffering, death, and even sin that hold men in bondage. But in all this he never ceases to be God the Lord. His person or being is constantly involved in change. Yet in all these changes God never becomes unlike himself. He remains Lord even amid the limitations of human life he has accepted in Jesus Christ. In the Biblical conception of God his unchangeableness is his unswerving faithfulness to his covenant. The unchangeable quality in God is his will of love, his desire for the redemption of men. But in fulfilling this will of love, God freely relates to his creation in different ways. The One who created the world is free to be a creature without ceasing to be Lord of all. There is no mode of being that God cannot enter.

Through the work of the apologists of the second and third centuries, the Biblical doctrine of God was brought into relation with the Greek philosophical conception of God. They sought to understand the dynamic, personalistic monotheism of the Bible in terms of an abstract and static conception of the divine being. Hellenistic philosophical monotheism described the absoluteness of God as his changelessness. Because he is Pure Being, he exists forever beyond change or passion. Because God is beyond change or suffering or death, it is unthinkable that he could enter the earthly realm where change and decay abound. As Celsus had pointed out, the acceptance of passion or change in God was tantamount to saying that God was no longer divine. For the essence of divinity was its unchangeableness. God was the Unmoved Mover, in whose pure actuality no change was possible. As Pure Being, he stood beyond the realm of becoming and change.

There were important apologetic values in the use of Hellenistic, philosophical monotheism by the early Christians. It gave them a way of intellectually differentiating themselves from the polytheistic mystery religions that were often their rivals. It also gave them a way of defending themselves from charges of polytheism that were leveled by some of their Jewish critics. The use of a philosophical conception of God helped establish a bridge to the intellectual community of that time. But this use of essentially abstract and static patterns of thought involved the church in a nest of problems from which it never really escaped. For when God's absoluteness is defined in static terms as changelessness and his person is described as abstract being, a *rapprochement* with Biblical thought becomes impossible. This abstract, static conception of God does not provide a means of making intelligible the divine presence in Jesus Christ, a human being who shares fully in change and even death. Nowhere is this problem seen more clearly than in what happened to the kenosis motif during these crucial centuries in the life of the church.

Kenosis Doctrine in the Early Fathers

The kenosis motif seems to have played a lively part in the Christology of the second century. Although there was no fully developed kenotic Christology at that time, there appeared in much Christian piety a naïve, nonspeculative type of kenosis doctrine to explain what God had done in Christ. The basic conviction that the perfect revelation of God, who is beyond history, is found in Jesus Christ, a historic person, led to the conception that God in some way limited himself in this revelation. In his *Letter to Polycarp* 3:2, Ignatius (d. 115) said:

Be on the alert for him who is above time, the Timeless, the Unseen, the One who became visible for our sakes, who was beyond touch and passion, yet who for our sakes became subject to suffering, and endured everything for us.

Similarly, Hippolytus (ca. 170–ca. 235) said that the Father was no longer satisfied to proclaim his Word obscurely, so the Father sent forth the Logos " that we could see him with our own eyes." The Logos was now " corporeally present among us." The Logos received a body from a virgin and participated fully in every state of this life being " of the same nature with ourselves " (*The Refutation of All Heresies* X. xxix). He accepted fully the sufferings of this life and even death itself. " And the impassible (*apathōs*) Logos of God went under suffering (*pathos*)." (*Against Noetus* XV.) Popular piety of that time had no reserve about speaking of Jesus Christ as " our God " or of his death as " the passion of my God " (Ignatius, *Letter to the Ephesians* 18 and *Letter to the Romans* 6). It was such a naïve statement of the kenosis motif that drew the scorn of Celsus. Celsus charged the Christians with teaching that God, an Immortal, came down and accepted change. (Origen, *Against Celsus* IV. 14.) Such a charge was not simply a calumny devoid of factual basis. Early Christian piety still conceived of the divine action in Christ in dynamic categories of understanding like those of the New Testament itself. It was not restricted by a rigid doctrine of the divine changelessness.

However, already in Irenaeus (ca. 130–ca. 200) the influence of a more philosophically sophisticated but less dynamic idea of God is seen in his interpretation of kenosis. Irenaeus stressed the eternal coexistence of the Logos with the Father. Because the Logos is divine, the Logos is thereby immutable. The Logos could descend to take up his dwelling in a human life. But the work of the Logos was limited to those activities that were compatible with divinity.

For just as he was man in order that he might be tempted, so too he was Logos in order that he might be glorified. When he was being tempted and crucified and dying, the Logos remained quiescent; when he was overcoming and enduring and performing deeds of kindness and rising again and being taken up, the Logos aided the human nature. (*Against Heretics* III. xix. 3.)

The center of emphasis has now shifted. The divine kenosis is no longer a change in the divine mode of being. Such a change is really not possible. The kenosis is rather the act of the Logos in accepting a human vesture. The Logos does not participate fully in the life of Christ, but only in those parts which are appropriate to deity.

Origen (ca. 185–ca. 254) accepted the kenotic motif into his Christological thought. He took it to be part of the apostolic message. (*De principiis*, Pref. 4; I. ii. 8; *Against Celsus* IV. 5 and 14.) But he is clear that kenosis does not imply any change in the Logos. "For, continuing unchangeable in his essence, he (Logos) condescends to human affairs by the economy of his providence." (*Against Celsus* IV. 15.) The actual emptying consists in the Logos' taking up a human life. Origen advanced two suggestions as to why this kenosis is necessary. He says that the very magnitude of God keeps us from seeing him. It is only as we contemplate him on a small scale that we can know him. He used the figure of a huge statue that fills the whole world as an illustration. Its very magnitude keeps it from being seen. We can gain some idea of it only if we see a small copy made in the same material. (*De principiis* I. ii. 8.) Origen also suggested that the kenosis means a veiling of the "splendors and brilliancy of deity" that men may have their first faltering glimpse of the divine. "He becomes as it were flesh, speaking with a literal voice, until he who received him in such a form is able, through being elevated in some slight degree by the teaching of the Word, to gaze upon what is his real and preeminent appearance." (*Against Celsus* IV. 15.)

Kenosis and the Resolution of the Arian Controversy

During the Arian controversy, in the period leading up to the Council of Nicaea, the reinterpretation of the kenosis motif already under way was given its decisive form. The Arians had played on the ambiguity of the phrase " in the form of God" as a characterization of Christ. They had argued with some cogency that to be " in the form of God " meant that the Christ was a semidivine or angelic being. He had been created by God the Father " in the form of God." To answer this argument, Victorinus (*Against the Arians* 1.9, 13, and 23) and other orthodox exegetes claim that " in the form of God " means the same as the Logos which is coeternal with the Father. To be " in the form of God " implies all that was subsequently embodied in the concept of the Second Person of the Trinity. The phrase " in the form of God " was to be rid of all ideas of subordination. The status of the Christ is the same before and after the earthly life. There is no exaltation to a higher form of life in the resurrection-ascension. Such a change is an impossibility because the Christ is already fully divine.

In addition to the work of Victorinus, Athanasius is also determinative for all future understanding of the kenosis. Athanasius went to great lengths to show that there could be no emptying or loss of the divine nature during the earthly life of Jesus. Athanasius based his argument on the deification theory of salvation, a theory then current in the church. According to this theory, men are saved from the power of sin and death by the deification of their flesh. Through grace the mortal or fleshly element in man is changed into an immortal substance thus giving him eternal life. Christ is the Savior of mankind because of his power to deify the fleshly or mortal element in men. This power in Christ is based on his fully divine nature. So Athanasius argued in his *Incarnation of the Word of God* that Christ can be Savior only if God is really and fully present in him. Any diminution or change in the divine nature in Christ would vitiate his power to be a Savior for mankind. No semidivine being could work this miracle of salvation. It could only be accomplished through the undiminished presence of God in Christ at all times, including his earthly ministry. The unchangeableness of the divine nature in Christ is the assurance of salvation. To envisage a change in it would be to foreclose the possibility of redemption. This meant that Athanasius could recognize no kenosis or exaltation in the New Testament sense. (*Speeches Against the Arians* i. 37, 38, 40, 42, 43, 45.)

The triumph of the Athanasian position and the subsequent development of the doctrine of the two natures in Christ rendered further use of the kenotic motif in Christology problematic. The kenosis motif lost its constructive role in Christological thinking. It was increasingly interpreted within the narrow limits set by the doctrine of the divine immutability. This can be seen in the work of Hilary (ca. 315-367) on the kenosis in his *Treatise on the Trinity* IX. 14; XI. 48; and XII. 6. His statements are often ambiguous and contradictory. The renunciation of the "form of God" goes just far enough to make the assumption of the "form of a servant" possible. But the renunciation does not go so far that Christ does not continue to be Christ. The "form of God" is not involved in the "obedience unto death." Similarly, the "form of God" is not inherent in the "form of a servant." (IX. 14.) Yet through "the mystery of the gospel dispensation" the same person is in both. The change of "fashion" (*habitus*, i.e., outward visible guise) that the body denotes and the acceptance of human nature does not destroy the divine in him. "The emptying of the form does not then imply the abolition of the nature." (IX. 14.) The renunciation of the "form of God" is a continuous process. He is constantly tempering himself to the human form. It is as if the divine nature threatened to leap over the bounds of humanity. Yet while under the wrap of humanity the divine nature is at work for the benefit of mankind because it is Christ's absolute possession. (XI. 48.)

In a sermon on Matt. 19:1, Gregory of Nazianzus (329?-?389) used the kenotic motif. His statements are rhetorical and paradoxical rather than systematic. Gregory was describing the work of Christ in terms of the recapitulation theory. Christ has lived through every stage of human life. This is possible because of the self-emptying of Christ that allows him to enter all the stages of life and its sufferings to sanctify them. Yet in this self-emptying and assuming of human form, he does not lose the unity of his person.

What he was he laid aside; what he was not he assumed; not that he became two, but he deigned to be One made of two. He removeth from place to place, who is not contained in any place the timeless, the bodiless, the uncircumscript, the same who was and is, who was both above time, and come under time, and was invisible and is seen. (*Orations* XXXVII. 2.)

Gregory advanced another reason for the divine self-emptying; like Origen he saw it as an accommodation to human weakness. Men cannot comprehend Christ in his full glory. "He strips himself for us. . . . By this he becomes comprehensible to us." (XXXVII. 3.)

Cyril of Alexandria (d. 444) utilized the kenotic motif in the development of his Christology. He found the kenotic idea helpful in his struggle against the Antiochian Christology. The Christology of the school of Antioch placed strong emphasis on the reality of Christ's humanity. But it found no adequate way to comprehend the unity of Christ. Cyril in opposition held strongly for the unity of Christ's person. The unity of Christ's person is only possible, he argued, if the Logos actually became man, not merely assumed manhood. The Antiochians, Cyril claimed, actually hold for an exaltation of the human subject in their view of the incarnation. The God-inspired man Jesus was exalted to the role of Christ. Cyril claimed that this was not what the church or Scriptures taught. The true teaching was that the "Word became flesh." This means a limitation or kenosis of the Divine Subject rather than the exaltation of the human. Christ freely accepted this limitation which allowed him to enter fully upon human life to redeem it. (*Against Theodoret*, Ananthema iii and x, tom. ix.) The kenosis is the voluntary subjection to the laws of physical growth, hunger, thirst, weariness, etc. (*Against Nestorius* I. 1.) Cyril is considerably less clear on the extent to which Jesus is subject to the laws of normal human existence in his intellectual and moral life. Actually the Logos itself could not be limited in knowledge. Jesus only seemed to be ignorant because a limitation of knowledge is appropriate to human life. (*To the Rulers* XVI.) Like Origen, Cyril really understood the kenosis as the acceptance of a human guise by the Logos. Jesus' limitations were real in the physical realm where they did not touch the moral and intellectual life of the Logos. Using the illustration of the heat in a piece of glowing iron that is unaffected by a blow on the iron, he argued that the divine element (the heat) in Christ remains impassible amid the sufferings of the humanity (the iron). The divine in Christ is untouched by the sufferings of his human nature. In this way Christ can be spoken of as " suffering impassibly."

The very reality of the physical life of Jesus is further called into question by Cyril's doctrine of the *communicatio idiomatum,* or the sharing of attributes. Cyril sought to explain the unity of Christ's person by means of a sharing of attributes of the divine and human natures. The human and divine natures in Christ do not merely coexist in the person of Christ; they interpenetrate one another. Thus in the incarnation the flesh of Christ is endowed with life-giving power because it is caught up in the divine. (*Against Nestorius* IV. 5.) The humanity of Jesus is deified so the human nature is swallowed up in the divine. (*Thesarus,* assertion 28.) The divine nature imparts its attributes to the human nature. But because of the impassibility of the divine, it can receive no attributes from the human nature. There is a deification of the human, but no humanization of the divine. So although there is a clear doctrine of kenosis in certain aspects of Cyril's teaching, the kenosis is finally qualified to the point where it implies no real limitation of the divine being. Kenosis for Cyril means the acceptance of a human vesture. Yet even this vesture is subsequently glorified.

The kenosis motif finds expression also in the thought of

Apollinarius (ca. 310–ca. 390), who was subsequently condemned as a heretic. He was struggling with the problem of
understanding the relation of God, who is immutable, to a
finite, human life. For him the problem was set in its most
acute form because he rejected all dualism between the human
and the divine natures that kept them disconnected except by
influence. His thought was developed in conscious opposition
to the Antiochian school. In Apollinarius' Christology the immutable Logos, which is fully divine, became the integrating
core of the finite human personality of Jesus. The Logos took
the place of the human spirit in Jesus. This most intimate union
between the immutable Logos and the mutable human person
of Jesus was made possible by an act of self-limitation or kenosis.
Apollinarius writes in the *Contra Diodorum:* " Incarnation is
self-emptying and the self-emptying revealed him who emptied
himself to be not man but Son of Man, by way of limitation
not of change." [10] This self-limitation of the Logos is explained
by a distinction between Christ's divine nature as it coexists
with the Father and that same nature under the conditions of
the incarnation.

In the incarnate life the Logos is inferior to and estranged
from the glories of the divine life. In this respect it is limited.
Yet the unlimited divine power is not totally absent from Jesus.
It can come into play. " Evidently it depends upon his heavenly
will whether Christ suffers or not, just as it depends on the
presence or absence of light whether man sees or not." [11] By
making this distinction between the limited and unlimited action of the Logos in the life of Jesus, Apollinarius hoped to give
reality to Jesus' moral and spiritual struggles. When the action
of the Logos is limited, Jesus' will can operate independently
from the Father. There can even be an opposition to the will
of the Father as there was, for example, in the beginning of
Jesus' prayer in the Garden of Gethsemane. His will put forth
power in its divine or unlimited aspect to accept death. But in
its incarnate or limited aspect it shrank from death. Thus the
earthly life of Jesus is not explained as an alternation between

the divine and human natures of this person in which the humanity is the source of his sufferings and his divinity the source of his triumphs over suffering. For Apollinarius the distinction is between the limited and unlimited action of the Logos. He wished to ensure the reality of the human life by a limitation in the activity of the Logos. In this respect his Christology approached more closely than any other of the patristic period to the kenotic theories of the nineteenth-century theologians. His solution was ultimately unsatisfactory. Having previously denied full reality to Christ's human nature, Apollinarius fell victim to docetism despite his introduction of the kenosis motif. He is clear that the kenosis is not complete. The existence of the Logos is not circumscribed by its bodily existence in Jesus. "While dwelling in human semblance on earth the Logos of God maintained likewise his divine presence in all things." Jesus is always conscious of his divinity, although he freely accepts all the experiences of humanity.

Apollinarius is right in insisting that the problem of ensuring Jesus' humanity be solved in such a manner as not to endanger the unity of his person. He is correct in seeing that the reality of Jesus' human life cannot be explained by relating some things as actions of the human nature and others of the divine. This was the usual approach of those who followed the orthodox doctrine of the two natures. But in its place he used as an explanation the alternation between the limited and unlimited action of the Logos. However, such an explanation is just as artificial as that used by the orthodox. It also has the disadvantage of creating a duality in the Logos. The Logos is simultaneously present in all creation in its unlimited aspect and at the personal center of Jesus in its limited aspect. The duality of the human and divine natures has simply been replaced by a duality of the Logos.

The Legacy of the Patristic Age

The church during the patristic age did not make full use of the kenosis motif as the basis for its formal Christology. Rather, the orthodox Christology was formulated in terms of the doctrine of the two natures. Christ was asserted to be both truly human and truly divine. Yet in this no attempt was made to show how these two assertions could be related to the one historic person Jesus Christ. Thus, although the doctrine of the two natures was given full dogmatic status by the Council of Chalcedon in 451, arguments over its meaning continued unabated. The distinction between the picture of Christ given by the kenotic motif and that given by the orthodox doctrine of the two natures is clear. The kenosis motif speaks of an emptying or diminution of the divine being so there could be a true human life. The doctrine of the two natures speaks of a fully divine and fully human nature in one person. The basic picture in the kenosis motif is that Christ foregoes the divine being in some way to become human. The basic picture of the doctrine of the two natures is that of the coexistence of the human and divine in one person.

The question naturally arises as to why such an early, clearly authenticated New Testament tradition as that of the divine kenosis in Christ did not play a greater role in the Christological thought of the church. There are certainly many answers to this question. But the decisive factors in the subordination of kenosis doctrine in favor of the doctrine of the two natures are found in the work of the early apologists and the anti-Arian fathers. The introduction by the apologists of the Greek philosophical monotheism into the Christian doctrine of God marked the first serious limitation on the use of the kenosis motif. The final limitation came out of the attempts of the anti-Arian fathers to expunge the references to any limitation or subordination of Christ's divine nature from Christian theology. The rather hazy and uncertain picture of Christ's preexistence as a semidivine being " in the form of God " was not too helpful to the fathers in their struggles against Arianism. The idea of subordination that it contains is difficult to fit into the emerging patterns of Christological and Trinitarian thought that stressed the full equality of the Son with the Father.

The dynamic personalistic conception of God and the pre-existent Christ found in the New Testament was theologically ambiguous and unformulated. The fathers sought to systematize these traditions through their use of Hellenistic thought. But such clarifications caused a shift away from the distinctive modes of understanding God and his actions found in the New Testament itself. The status of the preexistent Christ was no longer expressed in such nonspecific terms as " in the form of God." Now the Christ was given a very specific relation to the Father as described in the Trinitarian formula. The Son was differentiated from the Father. He was designated the Second Person of the Trinity. Yet he was not subordinate to the Father because he shared the substance of the Father. This clarification had two effects on the function of the kenosis motif in the thought of the church.

First, since the Logos or Son is of one substance with the Father, he shares the immutability or changeless being of the Father. Because of this immutability, the Logos cannot really share fully in the experiences of Jesus. The immutable Logos can have no share in suffering, want, or change. Already in Irenaeus the tendency to divide the activities of the earthly life of Christ had started. The works of glory in which the immutable Logos could rightfully share were attributed to Christ's divine nature, whereas all experiences of want, suffering, or change were attributed to his human nature. In this context, kenosis is not the giving up of divine prerogatives or being. By the very definition of the divine being, such a change is an impossibility. On the basis of its doctrine of the divine immutability, the only meaning the church could give to the kenosis was of a condescension of the divine to the inferior human form in which it was to be veiled.

Second, the exaltation theme found in the earliest New Testament Christologies and in the kenosis passage was replaced. In the kenotic as in the early adoptionist Christologies, the resurrection-ascension represented an exaltation to a new and higher status for the Son. In the kenotic conception the new status of the Son was a reward for his life of obedience and humility. In the orthodoxy of Chalcedon this notion was dropped completely. The resurrection-ascension was simply a return to a previously held position of equality with the Father. The specific New Testament formulations of the kenosis motif were reinterpreted on the basis of the anti-Arian writings so as to make them proof texts for the doctrine of a fully divine pre-existence described in the Trinitarian formula. The three key expressions in Phil. 2:6-11 that characterize the divine dignity or status of Christ — " in the form of God," "equality with God," and " Lord " — were read as equivalents. No change of status for the Christ was possible. The exaltation connected with the resurrection-ascension was simply the revelation to all of the true divine dignity the Christ had possessed from all eternity.

The developments in the patristic age effectively excluded the kenosis motif from playing a creative role in formal theological thinking for many centuries to come. The references to the kenotic passages of the New Testament in theological treatises simply repeated the interpretations of Victorinus and Athanasius. Yet the kenosis motif itself lived on as a basic theme in sermons, liturgies, hymns, and devotional manuals. The moral and religious appeal of this motif of the divine self-emptying was clear and strong. It continued to shape the thinking of Christians about the nature of the life of faith. The literature of mystical piety in the Middle Ages shows how the kenosis motif was destined to live on in the life of the church. The creative influence of this motif was felt in new conceptions of the Christian life, if not in formal theological discourse.

The Kenosis Motif in Bernard of Clairvaux

The importance of the kenosis motif in the mystical piety of the Middle Ages may be seen in the writings of Bernard of Clairvaux. Bernard finds in the self-emptying descent of Christ from heaven and his subsequent ascent and glorification the pattern of the spiritual life. The descent and ascent of Christ shows the path to be followed by the soul seeking union with

God. The ascent of man's soul to union with God is now possible because Christ ascended. But since Christ is equal with God, his ascent is possible only because he had first descended.

But he could not ascend without first having descended, and as his simple divine nature did not permit him either to descend or ascend, he took up into the unity of his person our nature. . . . In this he descended and ascended and showed us the way by which we, too, might ascend.[12]

There is in all men by nature the ineradicable desire to ascend. But in natural man this God-given impulse is perverted into the pathway of self-affirming pride and presumption that only serves to drive men farther from God. This is the sin of Lucifer which Christ rejected. The only way in which men can truly ascend is first to decend in lowliness and humility. Men must accept lowliness and humiliation as Christ accepted it. Our imitation of Christ is first in his humiliation and then in his ascension.

The self-emptying of God in the work of human redemption is further clarified in the *Sermons on the Song of Songs*. Here the divine self-emptying is described as consisting in three aspects: assuming flesh, bearing the ignominy of the cross, and suffering death.

For this is not a simple inanition, or one which is only limited or partial; . . . Did he not endure the wants and infirmities of the flesh, the temptation of the devil, and the ignominy of the Cross; and was there not heaped upon them all the horror of his Death? [13]

Bernard sees the divine self-emptying as the means by which God places man in his debt. It is evident that the Creator could have repaired the fallen creation with less difficulty than this. After all, did he not bring the world into existence by a mere word? God chose this more arduous way to salvation in order to bring men clearly under his debt. In this way men would render to him the gift of thanksgiving. In the act of rendering thanks to God, men are drawn closer to him. By thanking God for his descent, man makes his ascent to God possible.

Bernard goes on to argue that men might pass ungratefully by the grace shown in creation, saying it was all done by a mere word. But such ingratitude was not possible in face of the arduousness of the divine work in salvation. Creation took only six days; salvation took over thirty years of suffering. As men behold such grace, their souls are led to praise and thanksgiving. When we express our gratitude, our souls increase " in love of the Bridegroom, our Lord Jesus Christ," and we are drawn to him. For Bernard the meaning of Christ is found in his ability to lead us into a saving union with God. By his descent and subsequent ascent Christ taught men how they too can ascend to heaven. The divine kenosis is the pattern for the true life of the human spirit.

CHAPTER IV

The Rediscovery of the Servant Form

THE KENOTIC MOTIF IN THE THOUGHT OF
THE REFORMATION

The Kenotic Motif in Luther and Calvin

The Reformation marks a major breakthrough in the interpretation of the kenotic motif. Through his study of the New Testament, Luther challenged the traditional exegesis of the Philippian hymn for the first time since the Arian controversy. Coupled with this, and of perhaps more basic importance, was his rediscovery of the servant form as a way of interpreting Christ. In both Luther and Calvin there was fresh apprehension of the reality of Christ's human nature. The Reformers turned attention anew to what the New Testament meant when it said that Christ had "emptied himself, taking the form of a servant." They saw the religious significance of Christ's full and real sharing in the servitude to suffering and death that marks every human life. Luther and Calvin each approached the question of Jesus' humanity from different perspectives and drew differing implications from it. But they both focused attention on the importance of Christ as Servant living a fully human life. In doing this, they brought before the church a truth that had been lost to the piety of the late Middle Ages.

By the time of Luther the understanding of Christ in popular piety had effectively obscured his humanity. The figure of Christ had become so closely identified with God in his glory and majesty, and so remotely with man in his servitude and sin, that Christ's whole religious significance was changed. Christ was no longer viewed as a loving Savior, but as a threatening Judge who moved with terrible wrath. He was pictured as sitting on a throne dispensing judgment and condemning the bulk of humanity to the flames of hell while reserving mercy for a few souls. It was only because of his mother's fervent intercessions that his wrath was stayed at all. Christ was known only " in the form of God," and the " form " was that of a terrible and wrathful God. Christ was a figure of glory and majesty, not one who shared the miserable state of mankind. There was no point of contact between this Christ and a sinful man save through the mediation of the saints.

This was the religious outlook under which Luther lived during his early years. Luther came to question this conception of Christ because of the religious crisis in his own life. As he tried to live the Christian life as conceived in late medieval piety, he recognized the total inadequacy of its conception of Christ. This motivated his study of the New Testament, and out of this study he came to the fresh realization that the Christ in the New Testament was a Savior who had " shared our griefs and carried our sorrows." Christ is the Savior of mankind, not because he sits on a throne in glory, but because he shared fully in what mankind shares — weakness, suffering, and death. Christ is Savior, Luther declared, precisely because he was a helpless babe and finally a dying man on the cross. Christ had " emptied himself, taking the form of the servant." Luther recaptured the religious significance of the servant form and with it the importance of the divine self-emptying.

In his earliest writings Luther followed the traditional patterns of thought on the kenotic motif. He took the Philippian passage as a proof text for the doctrine of the two natures of Christ. But by 1520 he developed a new interpretation of kenosis that reflects his new understanding of Christ and his work. Up to that time, with few exceptions, it was assumed that the subject of the self-emptying mentioned in Phil. 2:6 was the preexistent Christ alone. The divine self-emptying was simply an explanation of how the incarnation was possible. Now

Luther broadened the application of the notion of self-emptying. The subject of the divine self-emptying was not only the
preincarnate Logos but also Christ during his earthly ministry.
Divine self-limitation occurred throughout Christ's ministry as
a man. The kenotic motif is used by Luther to relate his belief
in the changeless deity of Christ to his equally strong belief in
Christ's life as a frail human being. The central question around
which he developed his interpretation of kenosis was: How can
the glorious Son of God also be the man on the cross?

Luther arrived at his answer to this question by distinguish-
ing between the terms " form of God " and " divine essence "
in his description of Christ. Since the patristic age, these two
expressions had been taken to be equivalent. Now Luther said
having the " form of God " meant acting in outward relations
to others as God. The " divine essence," on the other hand,
is a secret, hidden, internal reality that may or may not be
expressed. " The form of God consists in this, that one places
himself as a God, and thus he acts, or takes upon himself
divinity . . . which does not happen hiddenly by himself but
before others." [14] Since Christ possesses the " divine essence,"
he can rightfully hold the " form of God." But if anyone else
seeks to assume the " form of God " without having the " divine
essence," he would be guilty of pride and arrogance in Satanic
dimensions.

On the basis of this distinction, Luther described kenosis as
Christ's constant surrendering during his earthly ministry of the
" form of God " for the " form of a servant." In doing this,
Christ did not lose or diminish the " divine essence." Rather,
to bring salvation to men, Christ gave up what was rightfully
his — " the form of God " — to live in full identity with those
he came to save. In order to serve mankind with the saving
power of his "divine essence," he " did not make a show"
(*prangete*) of it; " as a wise man holds back his wisdom in order
to serve a fool, so Christ withheld his divine glory to serve
us." [15] The hidden, inner reality of Christ's " divine essence "
remains at work even while obscured by the servant form. In

this way Christ can be Savior and still be the Suffering Servant with whom men can identify.

Luther describes Christ's existence in terms of two states: the state of exinanition and the state of exaltation. Christ's earthly ministry is carried out in the state of exinanition or humiliation. This is the kenotic state in which Christ freely accepted the "form of a servant." When his earthly ministry is finished, Christ is exalted by the Father in his resurrection and ascension to the state of glory in which he resumes the "form of God." In this state of exaltation Christ has his continuing or heavenly ministry as the Mediator for the faithful. The exaltation of Christ discloses his true nature, which he had veiled during the earthly ministry. This disclosure makes it clear to all men that Christ is to be worshiped and glorified as God, even though he had lived a life of humiliation and suffering.

The radical nature of Christ's self-emptying in the state of exinanition was a favorite and oft-repeated theme of Luther's preaching. In a sermon on the Nativity, he strikingly draws the contrast between the utter helplessness and poverty of the infant Jesus and his true status as Lord of all.

Behold Christ lying in the lap of his mother. . . . Look at the child, knowing nothing. Yet all that is belongs to him. . . . Your conscience would not fear but take comfort in him.[16]

The Christ who is Lord of all passed most of his life in absolute obscurity. No one knew he was the Christ. His redemptive work, which started with his baptism, was completed in his passion and death where his utter helplessness reached its height. Christ had so fully taken upon himself the "form of a servant" that he felt himself under the judgment of God when like a condemned sinner he hung on the cross.

This complete exinanition on the part of Christ was a source of comfort to sinful men as they came to know him. Seeing the Christ in his helplessness and suffering, men knew he came not as a Judge but as a Savior. He is a Savior to men because although he possessed the divine essence, he divested himself of the dignities and glories that were rightfully his to meet men in their weakness and sin.

Now is overcome the power of sin, death, hell, conscience and guilt, if you come to this gurgling Babe and believe that he is come, not to judge you, but to save.[17]

The significance of the self-emptying of Christ was that through it he could share the form of life of every man. In his lowliness he had brought the healing, redeeming power of God to men.

In his interpretation of the kenosis motif, Calvin proceeded from perspectives and concerns different from those of Luther. Calvin's approach to kenosis as to other Christological themes is dominated by his wish to keep the divine and human natures in Christ clearly distinct. He rejects out of hand any Christology based on a blending or transmutation of the divine and human natures. The divine and human can never merge. The distinction between them is absolute. It is not only the difference between the Holy God and sinful man. It is also the distinction between the infinitude of God and the finitude of man. This distinction has two effects on Calvin's Christology: (1) He emphasizes the reality and integrity of Christ's human nature. Hence, Calvin can speak of Christ's acceptance of the servant form in the most realistic manner. The Servant Lord can share fully in the servitude to suffering and death of his people because his humanity was real. It was not humanity transmuted or deified into something that was not really human. As Calvin repeatedly asserted, the promised blessing of Christ was " neither in heavenly seed nor in a phantom of a man, but in the seed of Abraham and Jacob." [18] (2) However, in making this clear and absolute distinction, Calvin is unable to account for the unity of Christ's person. Having clearly distinguished the natures, he is unable to show how they could share in the conscious life of a unified person.

Calvin followed the traditional exegesis of the Philippian passage. The " form of God " was taken as a synonym for the Logos, the Second Person of the Trinity, who is coequal and coeternal with the Father. The kenosis is explained as an occultation or hiding of the divine glory through the assumption of the flesh by the Logos. Calvin goes on to add that the kenosis does not affect " what Christ was, but how he conducted himself." The divine nature is in no way diminished. What Christ laid aside in his incarnate life was the exercise of the divine majesty and might. " For whilst he might have displayed his divinity, he manifested himself in the condition of an abject and despised man." This hiding of the divine under the human was so complete that it even involved to some measure the mental life of Jesus. For although as God he was omniscient, as a man he suffered ignorance like any true man.

But he is called " the servant of the Father "; he is said to have " increased in age and wisdom . . . with God and men," and not to " seek his own glory "; " not to know the Last Day "; not to " speak by himself," and not to " do his own will "; he is said to have been " seen and handled." All these refer solely to Christ's humanity.[19]

Calvin accounts for all of Jesus' limitations in knowledge by referring them to his human nature. Yet in doing this he is involved in a problem for which he never finds an adequate solution. The limitations of Jesus involve the core of his person. They are limitations on his intellectual and spiritual functioning. If these limitations are relegated to his human nature alone, then it would mean the divine nature was not involved in the most central aspects of his person. Calvin is obviously not willing to make such an admission. So he must find a way of showing how the Logos can be involved in Jesus' person in such a manner as to be compatible with a real limitation in knowledge.

The only hint he gives of how Christ can be both omniscient and ignorant seems to be in a doctrine of the dual life of the Logos. The Logos is not totally involved in Jesus' person. The Logos has a limited existence within the human nature of Jesus. But the Logos also has an infinite and transcendent existence as the Creator and Sustainer of the universe.

Here is something marvelous: the Son of God descended from heaven in such a way that, without leaving heaven, he willed to be borne in the virgin's womb, to go about the earth, and and to hang upon the cross; yet he continuously filled the world even as he had done from the beginning! [20]

This is the point at which Calvin chooses to leave the mystery of the incarnation. He does not expand on this suggestion that the Logos has in some sense a dual life in which he is simultaneously limited and unlimited. This theme was developed later by some of the Calvinists of the seventeenth century. And in the nineteenth century this doctrine became a major feature in some of the kenotic Christologies.

Both Luther and Calvin had focused attention on the reality and importance of Christ's human nature. They had rediscovered the centrality of the servant form for Christology. In doing this, they raised again the question of the kenosis. But their treatments of the exact nature of the divine emptying were sketchy and enigmatic. Luther suggested the distinction between the "divine essence" that is not lost and the "form of God" that is set aside. Calvin seems to suggest a dual life for the Logos. But these suggestions are not pursued, and the question of the kenosis is left largely unanswered. So it is not surprising that as the theological breakthrough of the Reformation was subjected to systematization and analysis by its heirs, the problem of the divine self-emptying occurred again and again. In Lutheran and Reformed orthodoxy of the sixteenth and seventeenth centuries the kenosis motif is explored more fully.

The Christology of Lutheran and Reformed Orthodoxy

The main theme in Lutheran Christology of decisive importance in the growth of kenotic doctrine in the future was its emphasis on the unity of Christ's person. Luther himself had made this very clear. In his interpretations of the traditional doctrine of the two natures in one person, he put emphasis on the one person. All the activity and suffering of the man Jesus

are the activity and suffering of God. There is between the
human and divine in Christ a sharing of attributes, a communicatio idiomatum. " Out of the infinite God has been made
a finite and definable man." [21] This emphasis was a constant
point of argument with the Reformed who stressed the distinction between the natures.

Lutheran orthodoxy taught that the uniqueness of Jesus was
precisely in the way in which the human and divine were unified in his person. The Lutherans criticized the Reformed for
teaching that the Logos merely sustained the human nature in
Jesus and did not really unite with it. Lutheran theologians
taught that Christ was capable of receiving all the divine attributes of the Logos. Johann Brentz (1499–1570) held that
Jesus shared fully in the divine nature and so was omnipotent,
omniscient, and omnipresent. This full sharing alone equipped
him for his work as Savior of the world.

This conception of Christ's person, which took on such importance for Lutheran orthodoxy, was originally developed by
Luther in connection with his view of the sacrament of the
Lord's Supper. The real presence of Christ in the Communion
elements of bread and wine was possible, Luther argued, because the flesh of Christ so fully shared in the divine that it
had the divine quality of ubiquity or omnipresence. Hence, the
body and blood of Christ could be present on altars all over
the world simultaneously. When this doctrine was read back-
ward from a conception of Christ's presence in the Communion
elements into a picture of Christ's incarnate life in history,
confusion was confounded. But this in essence is what Brentz
and others did in forming their Christology. They started with
a conception of Christ in a state of glorification and from this
tried to deduce a conception of him during his earthly ministry. These orthodox writers were always left with the problem
of how to conceive a fully human life beset by ignorance, suffering, and death for a being who was at the same time omnipotent, omniscient, and omnipresent. Luther himself was able
to deal with this problem partially with his unique conception

of kenosis. The earthly life of Jesus was the Logos in the state of exinanition in which the divine prerogatives — "the form of God" — were laid aside. Hence, Luther could give great importance to the fully human life of Jesus as the very guarantee that Christ would accept men in their humanity.

Luther did not try to synthesize these various discordant strands in his Christology. As the orthodox writers attempted a systematic ordering, the problems implicit in his teachings became more glaringly evident and the solutions to them increasingly arbitrary. Brentz held consistently that the hypostatic union of the divine and human in Christ was of such a nature that it could be truly said: God is man, and man is God. The finite was capable of holding the infinite. The divine attributes in their fullness were infused into Christ's human nature at the moment of the incarnation. The only concession to the reality of Jesus' humanity was that he used the divine attributes in secret.

This doctrine assured the unity and divinity of Christ's person. But the reality of Jesus as a historical person was lost. Kenosis, in this approach, consisted solely in the veiling of the divine glory and the assumption by the Logos of a physical body. Yet this assumption in no way limited the exercise of the divine attributes. There was here no real emptying of the divine but only its secreting.

Martin Chemnitz (1522–1586) brought forward a theory that could more easily accommodate a belief in the reality of Jesus' human life. Chemnitz originally developed his views in opposition to some theologians — dubbed by the Lutherans "crypto-Calvinists" — who denied the doctrine of the *communicatio idiomatum*. But in his efforts to oppose them, Chemnitz conceded the necessity of accounting more fully for the reality of Jesus' historical life. Chemnitz tried to do this in two ways.[22] First, like the Calvinists themselves, Chemnitz emphasized the distinctiveness of the two natures in Christ rather than their unity. Chemnitz taught that the human and divine natures retain their unique characteristics even after their union.

Second, Chemnitz taught that the divine nature did not exercise all its attributes during Jesus' earthly ministry. There was in this respect a kenosis of the Logos. He explains this limitation by the distinction between the quiescent and operative attributes of God. The quiescent attributes are the divine eternity and infinity. These are not directly operative during Jesus' earthly ministry. Thus it is possible to conceive how Jesus had a limited existence in a physical body. For the attributes of eternity and infinity are precisely those which would vitiate the reality of Jesus' physical body. However, in this theory, Chemnitz makes no real provision for explaining the reality of Jesus' human intellectual and spiritual life.

The lines of controversy were soon drawn between the followers of Brentz and those of Chemnitz. Brentz held for the full possession and use of the divine attributes by Christ. For him the kenosis only meant that Christ used the divine attributes and carried on his world-ruling work as the Second Person of the Trinity in secret. Chemnitz also held for the full possession of the divine attributes. But he argued that all the divine attributes did not directly affect the human nature. For him kenosis meant that Christ did not use all the divine attributes during his earthly ministry. The quiescent attributes of eternity and infinity played no part in Christ's relations to others. There was in some small measure, then, in Chemnitz' conception a real kenosis or emptying of the divine in Christ.

The Lutherans sought to conciliate this and other controversies that plagued them with the preparation of The Formula of Concord in 1577. But the formula did not really clarify the matter. The main function of the Formula was to give creedal authority to the conception of Christ's person based on the doctrine of the sharing of attributes. The unsettled nature of the controversy is shown by the exchange that ensued between the theologians of the University of Giessen and the University of Tübingen. The controversy was over the presence and activity of the divine attributes of Christ during his earthly ministry.

The Giessen theologians explained the kenosis as Christ's willingness to lay aside the use of certain divine attributes during his earthly ministry. Because Jesus surrendered the use of certain attributes during his earthly life, it was proper to say that at that time he did not really possess the attributes. He simply possessed the power to have such an attribute. The attribute was in a state of potentiality, not full actuality. Christ did not, for example, actually possess omnipresence during his earthly life. But he did possess the power to have omnipresence if he willed it. Christ's willingness to retract the use of certain divine attributes from full actuality to mere potentiality constituted his kenosis or self-renunciation by which he accomplished the work of human salvation.

In opposition to this view the Tübingen theologians held that divine attributes are always active. It is impossible because of their very nature to speak of them ceasing to function for a period of time. The divine nature is by definition pure actuality. It does not cease functioning in this or that particular way for a period of days or years. For the Tübingen school, the kenosis that made Christ's earthly life possible was simply the secret use of the divine attributes. This controversy was concluded without actual settlement by the Saxon Declaration of 1624, which basically affirmed the position of the Giessen theologians.

The emphasis of Lutheran orthodoxy that was most important for the new developments in Christology was its stress upon the unity of the divine-human person. The unity of Christ's person was not thought of as an abstract logical unity between two natures that could not really come together. The emphasis was constantly upon a unified person who had been formed out of the two natures. But the way in which this unity was conceived by the doctrine of the *communicatio idiomatum* made it impossible to envisage a truly human life for Jesus. Even those who followed the lead of Chemnitz in his distinction between the quiescent and operative attributes of God could say only that Jesus had a finite body. His spiritual and intellectual life was always characterized by omniscience and omnipotence.

Another factor implicit in the Christology of Lutheranism that was to be of central importance for future Christologies was its understanding of the relation of God and man. The basis for speaking of the fusion of the human and divine in the person of Christ was the basic suitability of human nature for the divine. The old axiom, *Finitum non capax infiniti,* "The finite cannot comprehend the infinite," was set aside. The Lutheran concept of the God-man had as its starting point: "*Deus est homo et homo est Deus; totus homo est Deus.*" Such a conception implies a belief in a basic underlying unity between God and man. Brentz was clear that even sinful man can share partially in the divine attributes. The distinctive feature of Christ's sharing in these attributes is that it is complete. Human nature itself is a suitable vehicle for the divine. This possibility of sharing in the divine was given to human nature at its creation. The possibility, which reached its fulfillment in Jesus Christ, is an endowment of all men. The full implications of this idea were never developed by orthodoxy. But in the nineteenth century it was to have central importance not only for the new Christologies but for the view of man developed in romantic and idealistic philosophy.

The Christology of the Reformed theologians was of a different spirit than that of Lutheranism. They shared allegiance to the ecumenical creeds of the church and used much terminology in common. But the interpretations they placed on this common ground reflect different starting points and emphases. The starting point of Lutheran Christology was the state of exaltation, with its emphasis on the majesty of Christ and the glory of his flesh as seen through its presence in the Communion elements. Its methods were deductive, seeking to deduce from the state of exaltation the possibility of a true human life in the state of exinanition. The Reformed orthodoxy had as its starting point the state of exinanition with its emphasis on the reality of the flesh. It was more clearly historical in its approach. The focal point of these differences is found already in Calvin, who insisted that divinity and humanity can never merge. The ruling axiom for Reformed Christology was to be *finitum non capax infiniti*. The problem in Christology shifted from that of Lutheranism of how to conceive a truly human life for the incarnate Deity to that of how to conceive the union between the divine and human.

The Reformed conceived of the incarnation as a *unio personalis*. By this they meant that the divine and human natures are united in the person of Christ. But when it came to explaining this union, the Reformed theologians became exceedingly subtle and enigmatic. How can the human and divine natures be unified if by definition the infinitude and perfection of the one excludes the limitations of the other? The answer the Reformed teachers gave was that the two natures do not share directly in one another. Rather, they can be said to share only in the person and work of Christ. The person of Christ acts as another entity standing alongside his human and divine natures uniting them. The natures, although not sharing in one another, are united by their common sharing in the person of Christ. The human is not pervaded by the divine, nor the divine by the human. Instead, divinity and humanity share in the one person of Christ so the attributes of both are present in him. By this approach the Reformed theologians hoped to ensure the full integrity of the two natures while also maintaining the unity of Christ's person. But such an explanation of the incarnation did more for preserving the reality of the two natures than it did for explaining the unity of Christ's person. The unity explained here is an abstract logical unity. It gives no ground for understanding the unified consciousness of a historical person.

The place where the unity of Christ is given a more convincing treatment is in the description of his work rather than of his person. The real unity of Christ is found in the cooperation of the divine and human natures in the work of redemption. According to Johann Heinrich Heidegger (1696):

" The function of Mediator Christ alone did and does according to both natures." The divine nature is able to enter this cooperative work with the human because the divine was in the state of exinanition.

He is the Mediator . . . according to the divine nature considered not absolutely and as it is common to the Father, Son and Holy Spirit, but economically considered, i.e., so far as according to it Christ submitted by a voluntary dispensation of grace, by receiving the form of a servant.[23]

To undertake the work of human redemption the divine underwent self-limitation, or kenosis. But the nature of this kenosis was not clearly defined. Sometimes the kenosis is explained as an occultation of the divine. At other times it is characterized as an actual limitation of the divine nature.

One of the most complete treatments of the kenosis is in the writings of Jerome Zanchius (ca. 1585). He taught that in assuming the form of a servant, Christ emptied himself of all divine glory, omnipotence, omniscience, and omnipresence.

He became from being very rich very poor, from being almighty, weak, from being omniscient, ignorant, from being transcendent, finite.[24]

Zanchius likened the kenosis to an actual retraction of the divine Logos as it took up incarnate life in Jesus. The Logos is retracted from a state of full actuality to one of potentiality. There was a true self-limitation or kenosis of the divine that made a human life possible.

This limitation of the divine made it possible to conceive a human life for Jesus, beset by weakness and ignorance. In this way the Reformed had a means of giving logical interpretation to one of their most often quoted passages: Luke 2:52: " And Jesus increased in wisdom and in stature, and in favor with God and man." On the basis of their kenosis doctrine they held that Christ during his earthly life was not omniscient. But he did have the power of discerning the truth. In this way it could be truly said that " he increased in wisdom."

And while we acknowledge that Christ as God was omniscient, yet as a man we confess that he was endued with knowledge great above all others, but yet finite and created, to which something could be added and truly was added.[25]

Similarly, as a man Jesus was not omnipotent or omnipresent. There had in this regard been a true kenosis.

However, the thought of the Reformed theologians about the incarnate Christ was always marked by a strange duality that the kenosis idea only tended to heighten. In their discussions of the incarnation, they distinguished between Christ as God and Christ as man, the former being omniscient, the latter in some measure ignorant. The Logos had in some respects limited himself in becoming a man. Yet the Logos remained infinite and transcendent. In this approach to the incarnation, it can only be explained finally in terms of a doctrine of a dual life for the Logos. The notion had been suggested by Calvin himself. But it was not developed fully until later when Samuel Maresius took it up again about 1662. He was quite explicit on the point. " Thus the Logos has united the human nature to itself, so as at the same time wholly to inhabit it and wholly to be outside it as being transcendent and infinite." [26] The Logos is both the center of the man Jesus and, as such, characterized by ignorance and finitude. Yet the Logos is also the Governor and Sustainer of the universe characterized by infinitude. But little was accomplished by this doctrine of the dual life of the Logos. It did not overcome the basic problem of Reformed Christology. It only shifted the paradox of how the human and divine can be truly united into the paradox of how a limited and transcendent aspect of the Logos can be united. The basic paradox for Reformed theology of the relation of the divine and human natures was not resolved but merely stated on different grounds.

Reformed orthodoxy made two contributions to the ongoing developments in Christology. Its emphasis on the historical life of Jesus as a person capable of suffering and ignorance was to be central, not only in the development of the kenotic Christologies, but in the growing interest in the historical Jesus. Many of the early Reformed theologians certainly did not develop this aspect of their Christology. For many it remained only an implicit assertion. However, by the end of the seventeenth century many Reformed theologians held consistently for the reality of Christ's actual ignorance and limitations as a human being. The other contribution was the interpretation of the kenosis as in some measure a real limitation upon the Logos. The Logos actually depotentialized itself partially in taking up a truly human existence in Jesus. The incarnation is the result of this emptying. Yet because of their firm adherence to the traditional doctrine of the divine changelessness, the Reformed were not able to fit the idea of a real kenosis into their doctrinal system. The often ambiguous and contradictory accounts of the kenosis in these writers witness to this difficulty. To enter a truly human life, the Logos had to limit itself, yet this is something which by definition it could not do, being divine by nature and hence impassible. Their only recourse in handling this problem was in a doctrine of the double life for the Logos. But such a solution was ultimately arbitrary and unsatisfactory.

The outcome of the work of the theologians of post-Reformation orthodoxy, both Lutheran and Reformed, was of ambiguous value. They were unable to arrive at a satisfactory kenosis doctrine. But through the rigor of their analysis they did formulate the question and problems involved in any kenosis doctrine with radical clarity. In this respect the work of these theologians may be viewed negatively as the exploration of the limits of thought about kenosis with the bounds of the Platonic-Aristotelian doctrine of being. The very fact that orthodoxy reached a dead end in its attempt to restate and systematize the Christology of the Reformers pointed to the need for new categories of theological thinking. The dynamic-personalistic picture of God implied in the kenotic motif could not be accommodated within the categories with which scholastic orthodoxy worked. In their rediscovery of the importance, both for the spiritual and the intellectual life, of the servant form for understanding Christ, the Reformers started lines of thought that went far beyond the confines of the systems of post-Reformation orthodoxy. The Christology of orthodoxy was another example of trying to put new wine into old wineskins. The result in such cases is a foregone conclusion.

The Kenotic Motif in Evangelical Piety

In the piety of post-Reformation sectarian Protestantism, the kenotic motif played an important role. The Pietists carried forward many of the unique emphases of the Reformers that were stifled within the formal church life and scholastic-type theology of the Lutheran and Reformed confessional systems. The religious significance of the humanity of Jesus and the importance of kenosis as the pattern of the Christian life are reemphasized in the thought of Pietists such as Count Zinzendorf, to which he gives expression in many graphic passages that seem reminiscent of Luther's preaching. For Zinzendorf the fact that the Logos, who is our Creator, became man is " the *coup de maître* of the Holy Trinity." This masterstroke of the divine action did not result in the creation of a great or glorified man. Rather, unlike the earliest prophets and teachers sent from God who could claim some status in the world of men — Isaiah was a prince and John the Baptist came from a priestly family — Jesus could claim nothing. When our Creator became man he came as a child, " a child, and indeed one poor as a church mouse, so naked that he could move a stone to pity." [27] All his life he spent as the comrade of the poor, suffering human weakness, finitude, and death. Kenosis, as Zinzendorf describes it, is not merely the submission to the physical conditions of human life. Kenosis meant a change in Jesus' own consciousness and the acceptance of human limitations in knowledge. As a child, Jesus had to learn the Bible and with it he learned " much rabbinic rubbish " because he was taught obedience and did not question the authority of his teachers.

It was only by the indwelling of the Holy Spirit in his life that he forgot the errors and only remembered the truth. And according to Zinzendorf, even in his miracles such as the raising of Lazarus, Jesus' weakness was evident. Jesus was troubled because he doubted whether he could raise Lazarus. So he prayed "as a child can pray now," because he was uncertain of his own powers. Jesus did not act from a sense of commanding certainty.

The kenotic motif was an essential link in Zinzendorf's interpretation of the Christian faith. He stressed a close personal union with the Savior who is also the Creator, Sustainer, and Redeemer of the world. Close communion with such a being is only possible because he had first become one of us. So now all men can have communion with him and share in his benefits. Here, Zinzendorf is echoing one of the basic assertions of Luther about the divine kenosis. The reality of Jesus' humanity is the assurance of our own salvation as man. But Zinzendorf did more than carry forward the insights of the Reformers. He added a distinctively modern element to his treatment of the kenosis. Zinzendorf explicitly relates the kenosis to the conscious life of Jesus. He extended the significance of the kenosis beyond the realm of the physical life into the realm of Jesus' intellectual and spiritual growth. He held that Jesus experienced growth and enlargement of knowledge in a way similar to all men. In doing this, Zinzendorf gave voice to a concern that has been central to all Christological thought to the present day.

The kenotic motif probably found its way into evangelical piety in part through the influence of Zinzendorf. The Advent hymns of Charles Wesley contain references to the kenosis. In the famous hymn, "Hark, the Herald Angels Sing," the coming of Christ is characterized as the emptying of the divine glory.

> Hail the heaven-born Prince of Peace!
> Hail the Sun of Righteousness! . . .
> Mild he lays his glory by,
> Born that men no more may die.

The same contrast is struck in another of Wesley's hymns:

> He left his Father's home above
> So free, so infinite his grace,
> Emptied himself of all but love,
> And bled for Adam's helpless race.

The contrast between the majesty and glory of the preexistent Christ and his lowly place in the incarnate life which he accepted freely is a theme in many evangelical hymns. An example of this is Emily Elliott's hymn:

> Thou didst leave thy throne and thy kingly crown
> When thou camest to earth for me; . . .
> But in lowly birth didst thou come to earth,
> And in great humility.

Such popular piety understood the kenotic motif as an admonition to humility and a life of self-sacrifice. These admonitions were based on the person and work of Christ who had forsworn the glories of the divine life to redeem men. Although formal theological thinking struggled and often failed to comprehend the kenotic motif, it found expression in the sermons, prayers, and hymns of Christendom. The emphasis on the personal, experiential reality of the divine self-giving in Christ that characterized evangelical piety was to leave its mark on the theological developments of the future.

CHAPTER V

Kenosis as the Bridge Between World and Word

THE KENOTIC MOTIF IN THE MEDIATING THEOLOGIANS

The Rise of the Modern Religious Consciousness

By the eighteenth century, orthodoxy, both Protestant and Roman Catholic, was under decisive attack intellectually and religiously. Intellectually, the rise of modern philosophy, particularly in its rationalistic forms in the Enlightenment thinkers, brought all supernatural religion under attack. The rise of the modern physical sciences destroyed the cosmology within which Christian revelation had traditionally been interpreted. And the growth of modern historical science called the historicity of Scripture into question. Religiously, orthodoxy was being challenged by pietistic sects that burgeoned throughout Europe. This pietistic, sectarian revolt provided ample testimony to the spiritual aridness of current church life. Although the full impact of this ferment was not to be felt in the realm of popular religious life for some time, a major corner had been turned in the growth of Christian thought. New questions were being asked about the faith. New ways of thinking were required for their answer. Both intellectually and experientially Christianity was being forced to rethink its doctrinal formulations and organizational patterns. The coming of the modern world posed for the church an intellectual task of dimensions unequaled since the patristic age. The orientation of Christianity to modernity is a task unparalleled in scope since the orientation of the faith to the Hellenistic world of antiquity. And in no place was its impact to be felt as decisively as in the understanding of the person and work of Christ.

The major shifts in the patterns of theological thought and church life that have characterized Western Christianity since the eighteenth century can best be described as the outgrowth of a shift in the religious consciousness of Western man. The modern reinterpretation of Christianity was not simply a matter of the adjustment or restatement of this or that aspect of Christian doctrine. Such adjustments and attempts at reformulation have always gone on in the life of the church. What was afoot was more nearly a change in the whole frame of reference within which men thought about themselves and their religious faith. A new form of human self-awareness was arising that can only be described as a new form of consciousness. The basic picture men had of themselves and of their world was being transformed. And because of this transformation, men were approaching the Christian tradition with new questions and new concerns.

The basic footings for this new outlook on the faith had already been laid in the Renaissance and Reformation. Yet as was seen with the Christology of the Reformers, the implications of their major breakthrough were never realized by their orthodox interpreters. Similarly, the roots of modern philosophy and historical science were already given in the Renaissance. But their application to the understanding of Christian faith had been stifled as heresy. The major reexamination of Christianity that was implicit in the Renaissance and Reformation only started to become fully explicit in the Age of Enlightenment.

It is impossible to characterize fully the complex changes that mark the formation of the modern mind. Its roots are clearly in the enlarging picture of the universe and of man's power given through modern science to transform that universe. Man had gained a new power to understand himself and his world. Man saw himself as central. The traditional picture of God presiding over a tiny geocentric universe was gone. In its place was one in which man sought to illumine the vastness and complexity of his world through his own rational powers.

Although the exact forms of thought and expression this new consciousness took in the Enlightenment were soon challenged and revised by the romantic revolt in art and philosophy, the central place of man in the universe and his awareness of his powers remained a dominant note for all modernity. It was the anthropocentric nature of the consciousness of Western man that was to be decisive for the growth of religious thought. The starting point for religious thought was not to be an unquestioned revelation given in Scripture or church dogma. For man had started to question and evaluate revelation by rational criteria and historical study. Revelation was to be approached rationally and experientially. Church dogma and even Scripture itself were reevaluated on these grounds. The whole Christological question was reopened in the most radical way. The interpretation of Christ in the ecumenical creeds, which had gone unchallenged by the Reformers, was now opened to question by the Unitarians and the Deists. They held that the traditional ontological interpretations of Christ in the ecumenical creeds had obscured rather than expressed the real Jesus. They sought in Jesus' ethical teachings the real core of his mission. Some of the German romantics by the end of the eighteenth century were maintaining that Jesus could be interpreted on purely historical grounds as a religious genius. Such were the new concerns being expressed about Jesus. And from them a myriad of new interpretations arose.

The problems envisaged in the reorientation of Christianity to the modern, anthropocentric religious consciousness are manifold. In the reconception of Christology the most basic changes came through the application of the critico-historical method to the study of the life of Jesus. From the very earliest beginnings of Christian thought the historical reality of Jesus had been asserted as a basic article of faith. However, the actual picture of Jesus that had come down through the life of the church was a mixture of the historical witness along with the myths, legends, and ontological theories by which Christ's meaning was interpreted. No systematic attempt was made to distinguish the historical reality from the many levels of interpretation given to Jesus in the New Testament and later in the dogma of the church. Now through the rise of modern historical method with its techniques of source analysis and the comparative study of mythology, it was possible to pursue the historical interest in Jesus in a new way. The new picture of Jesus, or perhaps it is more accurate to say the new pictures of Jesus that emerged from this type of study, revolutionized Christological thought. Historical study opened the possibility of reconstructing the life of Jesus as a concrete historical person and then of comparing this picture with that given in church dogma and Christian piety.

The full implications of the historical study of Jesus emerged only gradually. At first men simply became aware through historical analysis of a distinction between the picture of Jesus given in Christian doctrine and Jesus as he lived as a man in first-century Palestine. As early as the sixteenth century the radical sectarians such as Michael Servetus, Kaspar Schwenkfeld, and the Socinians demonstrated that such a distinction existed. They argued that the creedal interpretation of Jesus was a later development that misrepresented his role as an ethical and religious teacher. These men saw more clearly than their orthodox contemporaries the inability of the patristic formulas to express the humanity of Jesus. However, the importance of these discoveries were ignored in their time as heresy. Such considerations did not enter the main arena of theological thought until the eighteenth century. By the nineteenth century, through the work of men like D. F. Strauss (1808–1874) and F. C. Baur (1792–1860), the challenge to church dogma had grown to the point of a strident denial of the validity of the orthodox picture of Christ. The battle was soon joined between the proponents of historical criticism and the defenders of orthodoxy. In this struggle the kenosis motif was to play a vital role. For in the kenosis idea some theologians saw a way of reconciling the legitimate claims of historical study with the lasting affirmations of creedal orthodoxy.

The issue between orthodox Christology and the new historical picture of Jesus concerned the way in which his humanity could be conceived while still maintaining his divinity. Following the lead of Athanasius, orthodoxy had always tended to vitiate the reality of Jesus' humanity in the interest of preserving his divinity. While it is true Christians always rejected any Gnostic denial of Christ's humanity, no one had ever found a convincing way of explaining how Jesus could have a truly human existence. He may have a true human body in the traditional interpretations. But if his mind or spirit is really dominated by that of the Logos, it cannot be a truly human mind or spirit. A true human life, the historical critics maintained, is not marked by the omnipotence, omniscience, and omnipresence characteristic of the divine Logos. In fact, there are many passages in the New Testament to which historical scholarship made reference to show that Jesus experienced limitations and errors in knowledge. But almost without exception the defenders of orthodoxy rejected the possibility that Jesus' mind was prone to error or open to development. Such an admission they always said was a denial of his divinity. For the divinity of Christ meant that he shared fully in the divine perfections. Hence, creedal orthodoxy was not able to accept or interpret the fuller picture of Jesus' humanity that historical analysis of the New Testament was revealing. As this incongruity between the historical and creedal picture of Jesus became more evident, some followed the lead of Baur and Strauss. They rejected the traditional creedal orthodoxy as a means of interpreting the significance of Christ in favor of Romantic Idealism. They looked to the ontology of Hegelianism as the means of interpreting the significance of Jesus. Others eventually followed the antimetaphysical bent of Ritschl and interpreted Jesus as an ethical and religious teacher. Many remained defenders of creedal orthodoxy, unfortunately condemned to intellectual sterility and obscurantism. Some theologians tried to mediate between the newly emerging picture of Jesus given by historical study and the creedal affirmations of their churches. It is this group of mediating theologians who wrote the next chapter in the history of the kenosis motif.

The Problem of the Mediating School

The theologians of the so-called mediating school during the nineteenth century in Germany and Great Britain felt the necessity for uniting in their theology Christian orthodoxy, usually as interpreted in the doctrinal formulas of their own confessions, with the valid insights into Christian faith and history that were coming from the philosophical and critical historical studies of their time. Unlike the uncritical defenders of orthodoxy, the mediating theologians found much truth in the work of such contemporaries as Schleiermacher, Hegel, and the critico-historical Biblical scholars. Gottfried Thomasius, a typical spokesman of the mediating school, spoke often of the "destructive tendencies in present-day thought." Yet at the same time he clearly and repeatedly availed himself of historical insights and the logical forms of the philosophy of his day. Although the mediating theologians often differed sharply with one another on many issues, they were united in the desire to incorporate into the structure of Christian thought set by the ecumenical creeds and the confessional statements of post-Reformation Protestantism the valid insights of modern historical and philosophical scholarship.

The mediating school of theologians on the Continent numbered in its ranks some of the finest, if not always the boldest, minds of the time: I. A. Dorner, Gottfried Thomasius, August Ebrard, Bishop Martensen, and Ernst Neander. The mediating tradition was strong in the English-speaking world well into the twentieth century, claiming for its ranks most of the major theologians: Bishop Gore, Principal Fairbairn, P. T. Forsyth, and H. R. Mackintosh. Among their many differences these theologians were united in seeing the Christological question as the key one in relating the historical Christian confessions to the modern religious consciousness. Specifically, they saw

the problems of relating belief in Christ's divinity to their
equally firm belief that Jesus had a fully human mental, moral,
and spiritual life. The mediating theologians had accepted
from historical scholarship a picture of Jesus that emphasized
the reality of his humanity in a manner more radical than had
ever been done before. But they rejected the conclusions that
Baur and Strauss had drawn from this picture, namely, that
the traditional Christological formulas are no longer useful in
interpreting Jesus' significance. Rather, they set about the difficult task of incorporating the new historical picture of Jesus
into the earlier doctrines of the two natures of Christ and the
Trinity.

The Christological problem as seen by the mediating school
was the problem of understanding Jesus' mental and spiritual
life. The question had been raised in its clearest form for
theology by Friedrich Schleiermacher. It was usually called the
question of Jesus' self-consciousness. How could Jesus have a
limited consciousness, like all men, if at the same time he were
the Logos who shares the divine attributes of omnipotence,
omnipresence, and omniscience? One of the most fruitful answers to this question was first given by Gottfried Thomasius
(1802–1875) in a journal article modestly called, " A Contribution to a Churchly Christology." [28] Thomasius suggests that
the kenotic motif provides a means of answering this question.
Jesus could have a fully human self-consciousness because the
Logos had undergone a self-emptying in becoming incarnate.
In the transition from existence " in the form of God " to a
fully human life " in the form of a servant," there was a contraction or limitation of the divine being and, hence, of the
divine consciousness, that made a fully human life possible.
This lead was picked up by many mediating theologians and
enlarged upon in a variety of ways. For them the kenotic motif
became a principle of intelligibility in the construction of their
modern Christologies. Kenosis was an interpretative principle
that allowed them to resolve the problem of Jesus' human self-
consciousness and its relation to his divinity. Kenosis was to be

the bridge for relating church proclamation to the world. Its successes and failures in this role were tested in the vigorous theological debate that ensued throughout the rest of the nineteenth century.

The Christology of Thomasius

By the middle of the nineteenth century there had been a number of preachers, theologians, and Biblical scholars who had formulated kenotic Christologies in a fragmentary way. But it was Gottfried Thomasius, of Erlangen, who gave the first full and systematic treatment to a kenotic Christology in the mediating tradition. The starting point of his Christology was the affirmation of the kenotic motif as the key to a proper understanding of Christ. From this starting point his Christology went through an extended development from its first statement in 1845, until its final form in his posthumous works published in 1886. But the common core affirmation throughout was that the Logos in becoming incarnate limited himself so he could become the personal center of the man Jesus. Specifically, for Thomasius this meant the divine presence was retracted in such a way that there could be a natural development of Jesus' self-consciousness. His mental and spiritual life was not characterized in any sense by omniscience, omnipotence or omnipresence. Yet at the same time the Logos did not lose its fully divine nature while in this self-emptied form. In this way the incarnate Christ can rightfully be spoken of as truly human and truly divine.

The task Thomasius had marked out for himself was to explain the exact nature of the divine self-limitation that made all this possible. What changes did the Logos undergo to allow it to be the center of a fully human personality and yet still be fully divine? Thomasius advanced a number of answers to this question. But basically he followed two approaches: (1) He attempted a redefinition of the divine absoluteness that can take account of real change in the divine life. (2) He made a new analysis of the divine attributes so as to provide a way of explaining how the Logos can limit itself and still be truly divine.

In his earliest statements Thomasius described the kenosis as the laying aside of the divine glory by the Logos. Kenosis was not simply hiding the divine glory, nor was it a temporary and conscious renunciation of its use as described in the older Lutheran orthodoxy. It involved an actual renunciation of some aspect or mode of being of the Logos. On this point Thomasius was insistent from the beginning of his work. There had been a real change in the divine life to allow the Logos to become the center of a human life. By this insistence on the reality of the divine self-emptying, he challenged the regnant conception of the divine impassibility or absoluteness. Orthodoxy had taught that God was impassible by virtue of having pure and changeless being. By contrast, Thomasius taught that the absoluteness or impassibility of God is his ability to change and limit himself freely. God was no longer to be thought of as " motionless, dead substance; rather he is through and through will, life, *actus*, self-determining, willing absolutely self-powerful self." The absoluteness of God is not found, then, in changelessness but in his ability to change. God is most fully God in his power to modify himself freely, even to the point of limitation. The kenosis is the expression of God's ability to be fully self-determining in response to his will of love for mankind. No limit can be set to the activity of God other than the love of God. He is free to be the Savior of men by becoming a man. " The absolute might of God would be impotence, if it could not determine itself as it wanted and to what purpose it wanted." [29] Thus to argue that God cannot limit himself without ceasing to be God is to deny the basic meaning of the divine power — the power to be completely self-determining.

Thomasius summed up his new conception of the divine absoluteness in a formula he repeats throughout his writings. " Self-limitation is nothing else but self-determination." This formula is a statement in capsule form of Thomasius' whole argument about the divine absoluteness. (1) The highest expression of the divine nature is its power of complete self-determination. (2) This power of self-determination is most fully expressed in the self-limitation which made the incarnation possible. (3) Therefore, the self-limitation of God expresses his absoluteness rather than denies it. In following this line of thought, Thomasius had changed the grounds upon which the arguments about kenosis were to be conducted. Kenosis was no longer to be discussed in terms of a picture of the divine being as changeless. Now it was discussed in terms of a picture of God as capable of change. The divine being is described in terms of personal will. God is to be thought of as the only fully " self-determining, willing absolutely self-powerful self." Within such a conception of God the notion of kenosis as a real change in the divine being can begin to become intelligible. This new emphasis upon the divine freedom promised nothing short of a revolution in the doctrine of God.

But like many new ideas, this one soon ran into difficulties. As the new conception of the divine absoluteness was expressed in Thomasius' early writings on the kenotic Christology, a flurry of excitement and sharp disagreement swept the ranks of the mediating theologians. I. A. Dorner (1809–1884), who had early inclined to a kenotic Christology, launched a cogent critique of Thomasius' work.[30] Dorner claimed Thomasius' interpretation of kenosis had been developed without attention to the doctrine of the Trinity for which it posed insoluble problems. In the Trinitarian conception of God, Dorner pointed out, the divine absoluteness is rooted in the coinherence of Father, Son, and Holy Spirit. The members of the Trinity are so closely related to one another that a limitation of one is really a limitation of all. What happens to one member cannot be treated without consideration for what it means for all the members. So if the Son is limited in some way, then he is no longer fully the Son. And hence, the Father can no longer be fully the Father. Thus the kenosis as Thomasius described it actually vitiated the divinity of God. For if some part of the divine being is limited, then God is no longer fully God. While trying to explain the reality of Jesus' humanity, Thomasius had placed the whole doctrine of the Trinity in jeopardy.

Thomasius' critics urged another important objection to his work. It also had to do with the doctrine of the Trinity. If the Logos so empties himself as to lead a fully human life, what then happens to his world-ruling functions? If the Logos has become the personal center of the man Jesus, how can he be thought of as at the same time the creative and governing power of the universe? Such an objection is too obvious to be avoided. And it finally proved too difficult to be answered. There are certain absurd answers to this problem that can be rejected out of hand. Jesus could not be running the universe with one part of his mind while living a human life with another. This would leave him, for example, in the position of praying the Father with one part of his mind to calm a storm he had really started by direction of the other part of his mind. If the Logos had taken up a fully human life, as Thomasius explained it, he could have no conscious share in running the universe during the years of his earthly ministry. Yet if the Logos had retracted himself in this way, what keeps the universe from falling into chaos? No matter how helpful the kenosis idea proved to be in dealing with the problem of Jesus' full humanity, it posed such monumental problems for the doctrine of the Trinity. It was in the attempt to deal with these problems that Thomasius developed his mature position.

In 1855 the first edition of a multivolume work by Thomasius, called *Christi Person und Werk*, appeared.[31] These books were his attempt to answer his critics with a full-orbed treatment of the doctrine of God as the background for his Christological statement. If he was to vindicate his position, he had to indicate more clearly what was laid aside and what was retained by the Logos in kenosis. How could the Logos forsake the divine glory or " form of God " and still remain fully divine? Such questions led Thomasius to his second approach to the problem of kenosis: his analysis of the divine attributes. Following a lead given earlier by the Lutheran orthodox theologian Martin Chemnitz, Thomasius distinguished two types of divine attributes: the immanent and the relational. The immanent attributes are the attributes of God considered in and by himself. They are power, truth, holiness, and love. These attributes spring out of God's innerrelatedness as a Trinity. The relations within the Godhead between Father, Son, and Holy Spirit give rise to the attributes of power, truth, and love. The life of the Trinity as a whole is characterized by holiness. These immanent attributes reflect what God is in himself. For this reason they are the basic or essential attributes of God. They are what characterizes God as God. On the other hand, the relational attributes of God are omnipotence, omniscience, and omnipresence. These attributes are expressions of God's relation to the created order. The relational attributes are not essential to God in himself. They are the result of a relationship into which God has freely chosen to enter and from which he can withdraw.

Against this background the exact nature of kenosis can be explained more fully. The kenosis that makes the incarnation possible is the laying aside of the relational attributes by the Second Person of the Trinity. In kenosis the Logos gives up not only the use but also the possession of the attributes of omnipotence, omniscience, and omnipresence. In his incarnate life the Logos cannot be spoken of as having any of the relational attributes, only the immanent ones. What is gained by such a description of kenosis? First, it is clear the relational attributes are those which would vitiate the reality of Christ's humanity. No human personality can be thought of as being omnipotent, omniscient, or omnipresent. So the surrender of these attributes removes the greatest block to picturing Jesus as having a fully human conscious life. Second, since the relational attributes are not essential to the divine nature, their surrender involves the Logos in no loss of divinity. Even in this self-emptied form the Logos is fully divine. He still possesses

the immanent attributes. The Logos has simply withdrawn
from a relationship to the world into which he had freely entered in the first place.

But how about the immanent attributes of God? Would not
the power, love, truth, and holiness of God destroy the reality
of Jesus' human nature? Thomasius' answer to this was "No"
because the immanent attributes of God are capable of expression in and through a human personality. In keeping with
his Lutheran background, Thomasius held firmly to belief in
the power of the human nature to express the divine. Human
personality has a capacity for self-determination, love, holiness,
and the discernment of truth. These capacities allow a human
personality to be the means for expressing the immanent
attributes of God. For example, the human power of self-
determination gives a basis for the expression of the divine power in a limited but none the less real manner. Human love can be the means of expressing the divine love.
Human piety and moral obedience express the divine holiness. The human power to discern truth can be an expression
of the divine truth. In this way the essential or immanent
attributes of God can be expressed through a man without
vitiating the reality of human nature in any way. In their limited
form the immanent attributes do not preclude the limitation
of knowledge, the gradual development of consciousness, and
the bodily limitations that are a part of human life. Unlike the
relational attributes, the immanent ones can be adequately expressed within the limitations of human life.

This ingenious bit of theological speculation provided an
answer to some of Thomasius' critics. He was able to show how
the Logos can be both limited and yet fully divine. He was
also able to show how the divine nature of Christ is able to
be expressed through the human nature. But when it came to
the doctrine of the Trinity, he was not able to make much of
an advance. In fact, in his clarification of the doctrine of God,
he only tended to deepen the problem. For if the Logos goes
out of relation to the world, in giving up the relational at-

tributes, would not the world fall into chaos during the thirty-odd years of the Logos' earthly ministry? To this problem neither Thomasius nor any of the later proponents of a kenotic Christology was able to give an entirely satisfactory answer.[32] His rejoinder to the criticism was valid as far as it went. He said God had always been entering limiting or self-emptying relations. The creation of man and the world, the divine fellowship with men in every age and place, are all limiting relationships. In one sense kenosis has always been a part of God's activity. And these limiting relations have not destroyed God's world-ruling functions. According to Thomasius, God's entrance into these limiting relationships demonstrates his absolute power — the power to be completely and freely self-determining. God is free to enter any relationship with man and the world, even a limiting one, and yet not cease being God. The self-emptying of God in incarnation is the supreme example of the kenosis that has always been a part of creation and revelation.

As true as these observations Thomasius made about the kenosis of God in creation seem, they do not really meet the problem posed by his Christology. An answer to the problems posed by his conception of kenosis called for a more radical reconstruction of the doctrine of God than he had been willing to undertake. As a mediating theologian he felt the necessity for preserving the traditional Trinitarian doctrine of God. What he did not realize was that this is really impossible in light of his conception of the kenosis. He had construed kenosis quite literally as an emptying or loss of certain attributes. The Logos had given up omnipotence, omniscience, and omnipresence in becoming incarnate. This means inevitably that there is a resultant lack or diminution in God. Thomasius tries to account for this loss by arguing that there are certain aspects of the divine life that are not essential to it, namely, the relational attributes. These could be dispensed with, leaving the Logos free to enter a human life and still be God. But the traditional Christian doctrine of God had always held that there was nothing unessential in the divine nature. God's being is full actuality. This means there is nothing unessential in God that can be sloughed off. God is a unity, not a compound of parts — some essential, some unessential. There remains a basic incongruity between Thomasius' conception of kenosis and the doctrine of God to which he was trying to relate it. This was an incongruity that no amount of speculative ingenuity could overcome.

One of the boldest speculative attempts to relate kenosis to the Trinitarian conception of God was that of Wolfgang Friedrich Gess (1819–1891). Seeing clearly the problem posed by kenosis for the doctrine of the Trinity, Gess suggests that an administrative reorganization had taken place in the Trinity during the earthly life of Jesus.[33] When the Logos completely emptied himself to become incarnate, the Father handed over the world-ruling function of the Logos to the Spirit. Then when the earthly life of Jesus ends, the world-ruling functions are returned to the Logos. Such a dubious and bizarre conjecture does not provide a solution to the problem. Rather, it reveals the inherent impossibility of fitting the kenosis theme into the traditional Trinitarian conception of God. In the light of this difficulty two alternatives are open. (1) A new means of explaining what happened in kenosis must be found that allows it to be related positively to existing Trinitarian doctrine. (2) The doctrine of God must be completely recast so as to account for the possibility of a true divine self-emptying. The first alternative was taken by other theologians of the mediating school such as August Ebrard, Bishop Martensen, and later, P. T. Forsyth. The second, more far-reaching alternative was taken by theologians who were influenced by the philosophy of Hegel. They were the theologians of the left-wing of the nineteenth-century intellectual scene. They were more ready to break with traditional formulas than were their conservative contemporaries of the mediating school. Before proceeding to look at their work, we must give attention to the further attempts of the mediating theologians to provide a tenable kenotic Christology.

Kenosis as Transformation

J. H. August Ebrard, a Reformed theologian in Zurich during the mid-nineteenth century, also explored the kenotic motif as the basis for a mediating Christology. His interpretation of the exact nature of the kenosis stands in marked contrast with Thomasius. Ebrard appreciated the need for conceiving kenosis in such a way as to preserve the unity and absoluteness of God. He felt this could not be done by a conception of self-emptying that divided the Logos into essential and unessential aspects as had Thomasius. So he described kenosis as the transformation of all the divine attributes of the Logos into a form compatible with a true human life. In this way he avoided some of the pitfalls of Thomasius' approach. He explains kenosis as the transition of the attributes of the Logos from an eternal-form (*Ewigkeitsform*) to a time-form (*Zeitlichkeitform*) suitable to human nature. " The eternal Son of God gave up the form of eternity and in free self-limitation assumed the existence form of a human life-center, a human soul; he had, as it were, reduced himself to a human soul." All the attributes are still present, both immanent and relational, but now the attributes have a new mode of operation. They operate in and through a fully human life.

> For me Christ has not laid aside his omnipotence, omnipresence and omniscience; he did not need to because in truth omnipotence is not the ability to do everything, omnipresence does not mean being in all places, omniscience does not consist in knowing everything. For me Christ retained the essence of these attributes, that is, the power of Lordship over nature, the power of truly penetrating all objects, the Lordship over space. But he has these powers not in relation to the universe, rather he has manifested them in relation to single objects which he encounters in space and time.[34]

Such an interpretation raises to the ultimate point the problem of what happened to the world-ruling functions of the Logos during the earthly ministry of Jesus. For if the Logos is reduced to the form of a human soul, it could not very well be thought of as governing the universe. To this problem Ebrard suggested a unique, but not altogether convincing, answer. He suggests that the world-ruling functions of the Logos exist within Jesus but on the unconscious level. On the level of Jesus' conscious life the Logos had taken a limited, or transformed, time-form. The full actuality of the Logos in its eternal form as Creator and Sustainer of the universe exists on the unconscious level of Jesus' personality. In this way the absurdity envisaged by orthodoxy of saying that the man Jesus was actually in full conscious control of the world is avoided. And some way is provided for explaining the continuing divine government of the universe during the earthly ministry of Jesus.

Another way of dealing with this problem was worked out by Bishop H. Martensen of Denmark (1808–1884). He suggests instead of this division of the divine activity onto the conscious and unconscious levels of Jesus' personality, that there is an actual division within the Logos himself.[35] The Logos exists in its unlimited transcendent form ruling the world. The Logos also exists simultaneously in a limited human form as the Christ. The early ministry of the Christ did not interrupt or change the activity of the transcendent Logos. The government of the universe went on uninterruptedly because there is really a dual life of the Second Person of the Trinity. He exists in both finite and infinite form. Although this solution of the problem had been pointedly rejected by all the other interpreters of kenosis, Martensen held it was the inevitable outgrowth of the Scriptural evidence. Having speculated this far, he did not feel called upon to speculate further as to just how these two aspects of the Logos are related to one another.

In retrospect, this speculative theology of the nineteenth century seems of little more interest than as an antiquarian curio. The ingenuity of these theologians is always a source of amazement. But somehow their supposed solutions to their problems are never convincing. In trying to preserve the traditional doctrine of Christ and the Trinity, they usually end in mutilating beyond recognition the very thing they are trying to save. Here again is the proverbial struggle to put new wine in old wine-skins, with the inevitable result.

Yet no matter what their shortcomings, these theologians did mark a clear advance in interpreting the kenotic motif. They understood the humanity of Jesus with a new depth and reality. They also made a break with much that was inadequate in the traditional doctrine of God. From Thomasius onward they focused attention on the need for a reformulation of the doctrine of the divine absoluteness. These theologians saw kenosis in a fresh light. It implied a full and real change in the divine being. What was needed now was a doctrine of God that could relate such a change to the divine absoluteness. In their search for this doctrine these theologians reasserted the autonomy and freedom of the living God to which Scripture witnesses. They had taken a giant step forward. But their conservatism kept them from realizing its full implication. The mediating school faltered when it tried to rationalize and explain the divine freedom. Their rationalization became unconvincing speculations about the reorganization of the Trinity. The importance of their break with tradition was only to be realized by theologians of other persuasions. Of these, none were more intellectually interesting than the Hegelians who also left their mark on the history of the kenotic motif.

CHAPTER VI

Kenosis as the Key to Reality

THE KENOTIC MOTIF IN HEGEL AND THE LEFT-WING THEOLOGIANS

The Structure of Hegel's Philosophy

The philosophy of G. W. F. Hegel (1770–1831) provided one of the most appealing options for interpreting Christian faith to the modern world. In his philosophy Hegel presents a scheme of explanation embracing the whole of reality that gives a prominent place to the dimension of spirit. Not only does Hegel acknowledge the legitimacy and value of man's religious striving, he specifically grants to Christianity the status of revealed or absolute religion. In the century and a half since Hegel's thought took form the opinion of the Christian world as to its value has experienced a flood and ebb. Hegel's philosophy has been the object of much criticism both captious and just. Certainly existentialism and linguistic analysis, the regnant approaches in contemporary philosophy, call the whole Hegelian structure into question. Yet this should not obscure the fact that the philosophy of Hegel has provided one of the major vehicles for expressing Christian faith in the new intellectual climate that arose in the Western world after the Enlightenment. For the philosophy of Hegel was a bold attempt at synthesis between the main schools of thought in the Western world and major elements of Christian tradition. Although modern Biblical theology has adjudged Hegelianism deponent in its interpretation of Christianity as a historical religion, the constructive role of Christian tradition for Hegel cannot be overlooked.

Hegel sought to unite the insights of both the rationalistic and romantic traditions in modern philosophy. Following in the tradition of romanticism, Hegel took seriously man's ceaseless religious questing. But unlike such religious romantics as Schleiermacher, he was unwilling to justify human spirituality simply in terms of the experience of religious feeling. Rather, in the tradition of the rationalists, he sought for a rational structure to justify and interpret man's religious life. He tried to develop a logic that could encompass the richness and complexity of human spirituality as expressed in history, art, and religion. He refused to whittle down human spirituality until it could be comprehended by the limited patterns of logical thinking found in much rationalism. Rather, the underlying rationality of all orders of being and all forms of human activity including religion is to be discovered. "Philosophy," he says in his *Encyclopedia*, " is the science of comprehensiveness wherein the totality of Being becomes aware of itself." [36] Religion has a central place in this philosophy of inclusiveness. Religion was not to be limited to morality or reduced to feeling. It was to be comprehended out of the richness of its traditional forms and historic doctrinal formulas. The traditional forms and dogmas of Christianity are not simply to be rejected as obsolete or unintelligible. Instead, the true rational content of the Christian faith within them is to be discovered and reexpressed to the modern world. This is possible for Hegel because he believed he had found a logic and ontology that could encompass the complex and often contradictory aspects of religious tradition. Instead of limiting religion to existing modes of understanding, Hegel had evolved new modes of understanding more adequate to the substance of religion.

In the development of Hegel's philosophical and religious synthesis, the kenotic motif played a decisive role. In a manner far more profound and all-pervasive than that of the mediating theologians, Hegel utilized the kenotic motif in building his whole system of thought. To Hegel, kenosis was more than an explanation of Jesus' true humanity; it was the pattern of all reality. So when one is looking for the kenosis motif in Hegel, it is not sufficient to turn only to his treatment of the incarnation. The kenotic motif is found as the pattern of his whole logic and ontology. The kenotic motif is a recurrent theme in the whole of his philosophy. To grasp the basic significance of the kenotic motif for Hegel, it is necessary to understand his conception of philosophy and through it of reality as a whole.

In his *Encyclopedia of Philosophy*, Hegel describes the scope of philosophy. " In distinction from all other sciences, philosophy envisages the problem of *reality as such*." [37] The task of philosophy is to understand reality as a whole. In this effort, philosophy stands in distinction to the many particular or positive sciences that simply try to explain one part of reality in terms of another part. All the attempts to understand the world through the physical or behavioral sciences are limited to only part of reality by their very nature. For the sciences proceed on the basis of a cause-and-effect explanation. They use one aspect of reality, the cause, to understand another aspect of reality, the effect. As useful as such knowledge may be in certain regards, it cannot attain a knowledge of reality as a whole, or as Hegel calls it, the Absolute. What is needed for philosophy is a method of comprehending reality as a whole.

Such a comprehension or understanding of the whole of reality is possible because of the underlying nature of reality. The real is the rational; the rational is the real. This is simply a way of saying that the Absolute, or reality as a whole, and the minds that seek it are ultimately of the same nature. Reality as a whole is not alien to man's rational capacities. Viewed in their broadest sense, man's powers of understanding are an expression of that which they are trying to understand. Hence, the task of philosophy is a possible one. But the task of philosophy is not a simple one. This ultimate relationship between human understanding and the Absolute is not immediately evident, nor is its uncovering easy. The myriad and seemingly contradictory forms taken by reality as men experience it makes the discovery of its true nature difficult.

To avoid the modern caricatures of Hegel's philosophy, it is necessary to clarify what is implied in the notion of human understanding comprehending the Absolute. Such a claim does not imply omniscience. To comprehend the Absolute does not mean that the whole of reality is immediately or directly present in consciousness. This would be a kind of divine omniscience which even Hegelian philosophers do not claim. To comprehend the Absolute means to know its basic pattern or structure. If the basic pattern or structure of reality is known, then from it a systematic explanation of the whole can eventually be evolved. All the immensely rich and complex details of reality in its myriad forms cannot be known directly and immediately by a human mind. What a human mind can comprehend is the underlying nature of reality. The mind can comprehend this structure of the Absolute because it is of the same substance as the Absolute. Hence, the basic key from which Hegel develops his whole philosophy is his conception of the pattern or structure of reality.

Up to this point Hegel's work stands in the tradition of philosophical idealism of the Western world that stretches back to the Greeks. He is trying to discover the reality behind man's usual experience of the world. The significance of Hegel is in the basic change he brings about in this idealistic tradition. He realized that the weakness of the traditional idealistic ontology was its inability to account for the element of change or becoming that is so clearly a part of the world men experience. Traditional ontology said that ultimate reality is changeless being. The world of change or becoming is a lower order of reality whose relation to the ultimate is uncertain or accidental. In contrast, Hegel claimed that the basic nature of reality is not static but dynamic. The basic idea of logic and ontology for Hegel is the idea of "world-totality as eternal movement." [38] But this movement is not random. The movement has a definite structure. It is a threefold movement described by logic as the movement of thought from thesis through antithesis to synthesis. This same movement is described by ontology as the relationship of being to nonbeing and both of these in turn to becoming. This is the basic pattern of reality from which the whole of reality can be understood. It is possible to see what this pattern implies by starting with the most general ideas in logic and ontology.

In logic, to think a conception through to its most clear and certain point is to find it engenders or implies its own opposite. This can be seen by considering the most basic category of ontology, the notion of being. Being is the most general idea that can be applied to all things. When the notion of being is rid through logical analysis of all its particularity or forms as the being of this or that particular object, it becomes a complete abstraction. Since the notion of pure being is no longer the being of any particular thing, it is an abstraction that does not really exist. That is simply to say that it is now really nonbeing. By means of logical analysis the notion of being is shown to engender its opposite or nonbeing. The notion of being has passed from thesis to antithesis, or in this case from being to nonbeing.

In the Hegelian scheme this contradiction does not have the final word. For Hegel points out that this movement of thought from thesis to antithesis is an important aspect of reality itself. Thought does not simply jump from being to nonbeing. Thought starts with the being of this chair or that table. It then moves by a process of abstraction to a more and more pure conception of being until it finally reaches that conception of being which is free of all particularity and is hence nonbeing. But as thought makes this movement, it describes an aspect of reality in which being and nonbeing are both present. This is the realm of becoming. Becoming actually transcends being and nonbeing because it embraces them both. Viewed from the standpoint of logic, becoming is the synthesis between the thesis — being — and the antithesis — nonbeing. Becoming represents a higher level of reality than either pure being or nonbeing. Becoming has both being and nonbeing within it and hence can be said to overcome or transcend them.

Hegel used this admittedly abstract and abstruse triadic pattern of thought to solve some of the most basic problems that confronted philosophy. On all the great questions in philosophy — the question of man's freedom and destiny, the question of God, the question of ultimate reality — human reason had run into contradiction. As Immanuel Kant had demonstrated, pure reason inevitably engenders antinomies or contradictions when dealing with these ultimate questions. But are these contradictions the final word? Hegel asked. His answer was " No." He saw the contradictory answers to which men had come simply as thesis and antithesis that point beyond themselves to a higher synthesis. Inasmuch as the evidence on both sides of a question is valid evidence, it simply points to two different approaches to the question. When the various approaches to a question are isolated from one another, they become dangerous and contradictory half-truths. Instead, these contradictory answers must be viewed together to find the underlying unity or synthesis that embraces them both. The thesis and antithesis are only partial stages in the unfolding processes of understanding. A synthesis can be reached when thought does not make the thesis or antithesis final. To make the thesis or antithesis the final word is to settle for a partial or imperfect view of reality instead of the richer, fuller view of the synthesis.

In seeking to unfold his answer to that most basic philosophical question — the nature of reality — Hegel wants to avoid the contradictions that had inevitably beset the great ontologies of the past. He wanted to avoid an ontology that is partial or one-sided. Hegel hoped to do this by constructing a philosophy that could express the threefold pattern he saw in reality. His philosophy has three major aspects that are related as thesis, antithesis, and synthesis. There are the logic, the philosophy of nature, and the philosophy of spirit.

Logic describes the basic or underlying structures of reality. Taken in and by themselves, the logical structures of reality are barren and abstract. These structures are the pattern of reality without the substance. Logic describes only part of reality. For this reason, logic is the thesis or first part of the total movement of thought that embraces reality as a whole. Actually, of course, the structures described by logic are embodied in the myriad of particular objects that make up the world of nature. The world of nature is the world as men experience it. It is the world studied by the empirical sciences. This world of nature is complex and often contradictory in appearance. It is the rich, variegated world of everyday experience. It is a realm which does not reveal clearly the logical structures that underlie it. It seems, rather, to obscure them. In this regard, it is just the opposite of the realm of logical structure. In other words, nature is the antithesis of logic. Although the logic shows us the bare bones of reality, nature overlays these bones with the complexity of particular things. But in Hegel's picture of reality as a whole, the contradiction between logic and nature does not have the final word. The underlying relationship between the thesis — logical structure — and the antithesis — the world of nature — becomes apparent when viewed from a higher level— the synthesis. This synthesis is what Hegel calls the realm of spirit.

In the unfolding of understanding, the synthesis between logic and nature is reached in spirit. Spirit is reality that has reached the highest level — the level of self-consciousness. The human activities of art, philosophy, and religion constitute the realm of spirit in which the structure and meaning of all experience becomes evident. Spirit provides a clarification of the meaning in the manifold and contradictory aspects of reality. Spirit is reality comprehending itself. It is reality come to consciousness. As such, the realm of spirit represents the highest and fullest state of reality. It is the synthesis that incorporates and transcends the partial views of reality given in logic or in nature. As such, spirit represents a fuller or higher reality than that discovered by logical analysis or by the study of nature.

What Hegel envisages as total reality, or the Absolute, is a process of interaction between structure and its embodiment in nature that gives rise to the dimension of spirit. In the realm of spirit, reality comes to full consciousness. Spirit is world-process becoming aware of its underlying rationality. Spirit is reality integrating the fragmentary and seemingly contradictory aspects of experience into a meaningful whole. This synthesis of reality into a meaningful whole is revealed in art, religion, and supremely in philosophy. On the level of spirit, thought and reality understand themselves as one and the same. The fact that the real is the rational becomes clear. The opposition that ordinarily exists between pure thought, as described by logic, and the world of nature, as described by empiricism, is overcome. It is overcome by philosophical insight that does not deny either logical clarity or natural complexity. Rather, the highest insight of philosophy is the discernment of a rational pattern within the seemingly disparate aspects of reality. The apparently contradictory aspects of reality are but moments in the Whole. The Whole of reality, the Absolute, is greater than and more real than any of its parts. This truth is the highest insight of religion and philosophy.

The threefold movement or pattern of all reality in Hegel's ontology is really the pattern of kenosis described in the New Testament. He specifically makes this connection in his *Phenomenology of Mind.*

Actual reality (nature) . . . and implicit being (logical structure) are two moments; and by the reciprocity of their kenosis, each relinquishing or "emptying" itself of itself and becoming the other, spirit (the highest level of reality) comes in existence as their unity.[39]

The interaction of logical structure and its embodiment in nature is a process of kenosis or emptying that results in an exaltation of reality to a higher level called spirit. This pattern which Hegel sees as basic to all reality is the expression in ontological terms of the kenosis movement described in the New Testament. The preexistence of the Christ "in the form of God" is symbolic of abstract being or logical structure. The entrance of the Christ into the realm of natural man, the taking "the form of a servant," is symbolic of the embodiment of these structures in the natural world. This transition from existence "in the form of God" to "the form of a servant" is accomplished by a kenosis. The logical structures "empty" themselves or lose their abstract infinity as they are embodied in the particular finite objects that constitute the world of nature. But this seeming contradiction between the "form of God" and the "form of a servant" is not the final word. Rather, this contradiction is transcended by a synthesis of the two. This synthesis is symbolized in New Testament language by the exaltation of the Christ to the new and higher status of "Lord." In philosophical terms, this is the coming into existence of the level of spirit.

So, according to Hegel, the process by which being reaches full self-consciousness, the highest level of reality, is kenotic in pattern. World-process, the Absolute, is described finally by the movement of self-emptying followed by exaltation to a new and higher level of reality. Hegel had adapted this New Testament motif describing God's action in Christ to become the basis of his picture of reality as a whole. But in the process of adaptation, Hegel makes an important differentiation between his understanding of kenosis and that found in the New Testament. In the New Testament the self-emptying and subsequent exaltation of the Christ have a historical character. Self-emptying and exaltation are directly related to certain historical events, namely, the life, death, and resurrection of Jesus. In the thought of the New Testament the divine kenosis is made real through contingent, historical happenings. For Hegel, the kenosis-exaltation movement in reality is necessary and logical in character rather than historical and contingent. Although kenosis may be expressed through the life, death, and resurrection of Jesus, its validity and importance is not bound to these events. The kenosis-exaltation character of the Absolute is rational and eternal in character. This process is perceived by mind as the inherent order of reality. The kenosis movement is not an event that happened at this or that point in history. It is the eternal pattern of all being in its emerging consciousness as Absolute Spirit. Since the whole of world-process is described by the kenotic motif, the self-emptying cannot be isolated at only one particular moment in the process.

Although the kenotic motif in ontology is ultimately a philosophical insight justified by its own rational character, its historic expression in Jesus is not thereby unimportant. The life,
death, and resurrection of Jesus present in pictorial form the
kenotic pattern of reality. The basic unity between God, or
Absolute Spirit, and man, or finite spirit, was revealed in the
person of Christ. These ideas did not attain to the rational
clarity and cogency they have in philosophical knowledge.[40]
The religious mind perceives truth in pictorial or imaginative
forms. Religious ideas are concretely embodied in particular
persons and historical events. The importance of the particular
person, Jesus, and events of his life was that in them was first
revealed the underlying unity of God and man. In the essentially
pictorial form of the story of his life, death, and resurrection this
truth has been mediated to mankind. In the historical accounts
of the incarnation the underlying pattern of reality was first expressed. And for many men it is only in this form that the truth
can be received and understood. Philosophy gave the truth revealed in Christ a clearer and more logical form. But the revelation of this truth through Jesus was an important step in the
growth of man's understanding of the Absolute.

Hegel's Interpretation of Christian Doctrine

The key to Hegel's reconstruction of Christian doctrine is his
unique view of the nature of religious language. His whole philosophy of religion hinges on his idea of religious language as
Vorstellungen or pictorial representations. The great dogmas
of the Christian church — creation, fall, incarnation, atonement,
resurrection, and ascension — are Vorstellungen. No single word
or phrase is adequate to render this term into English. A Vorstellung is the presentation form given to an idea. For Hegel, the
Vorstellungen can be said to be the form taken by truth that is
suitable for presentation to the religious mind. A Vorstellung is composed of two elements: (1) It has a rational or logical content. It contains truth about absolute reality. (2) It has a
concrete, particular, or historical content also. The truth that the

Vorstellungen contain is expressed through concrete, particular persons and events. For example, the philosophical idea of the underlying unity of God — Absolute Spirit, and man — finite spirit — is presented in religious language as the doctrine of the incarnation. For the religious understanding, the philosophical idea of the underlying unity of finite and Absolute Spirit is expressed through belief that God was incarnate in Jesus of Nazareth. This belief is tied to the particular events in the life, death, and resurrection of Jesus. The truth that appears to philosophy as necessary and logical appears in religion as dependent on a series of contingent, historical happenings in the life of a particular person. The dogmas by which Christians have expressed the true importance of Jesus — incarnation, resurrection, ascension, and atonement — have enshrined a proper understanding of reality. But this understanding has been enshrined in the form of quasi-historical myths or pictorial representations.

The proper understanding of Christian doctrine proceeds from the analysis of its language of expression. The task of modern philosophy of religion, as Hegel sees it, is not that envisaged by the Enlightenment thinkers, namely, the rejection of classical Christian dogmas as irrational and contradictory. Rather, the philosophy of religion must uncover the rational content in religious dogma. The proper interpretation of Christian doctrine will reveal in it the true or dialectical understanding of reality. The error of the popular religious mind has been to absolutize the *Vorstellung* or pictorial representation of the truth. The church has always mistakenly insisted on the literal acceptance of the historical particulars of the life of Jesus. But this is to confuse the pictorial embodiment of the truth with the truth itself. The path followed by the philosophical reconstruction of religion is the discernment and elucidation of the rational content of religious dogmas and history.

Proceeding from such a broad mandate for reinterpretation, Hegel moves with a sovereign freedom through Christian doctrine, often to the distress of orthodoxy in his day and ever since. In effect Hegel brings about a major simplification and consolidation of Christian doctrine. He actually coordinates as practically synonymous the doctrines of the Trinity, creation, Christology, atonement, and ecclesiology. He is able to do this because he believes all these doctrines in various ways witness to one truth. The rational content of all these doctrines is the same. They all reveal the structure of ultimate reality as the movement from being to nonbeing into becoming. The one basic truth of philosophy and religion is that there is a triadic or kenotic pattern to reality. Reality is a dialectical process that moves toward full self-consciousness as Absolute Spirit. This basic truth, no matter how expressed, is the true rational content of all Christian dogma. Christianity presents this truth as belief in the Triune God who becomes incarnate in order to reconcile sinful men to himself. Philosophy presents this religious content in nonmythical form.

The basic pattern within which Hegel carries out his reinterpretation of Christian doctrine is that of the Trinity.[41] Hegel sees the Christian doctrine of the Trinity as actually a pictorial representation of his own conception of world-process, or the Absolute. The relationships between the members of the Trinity describe in pictorial form the relationship between the three aspects of reality that Hegel describes in his ontology. First, there is the " pure dialectical essence of all Being." This is that dimension of reality described by logic. This is the underlying structure of reality that provides the basis for the finite world of nature. In religious terms this realm is called the kingdom of the Father. This realm is symbolically represented for religious thought as the First Person of the Trinity. When viewed in isolation from the other members of the Trinity, the reality of God the Father is incomplete and barren. Full reality for the Father depends on his relation to the Son and the Spirit. In this the Father is like the abstract, logical structure of the realm of pure being. These structures are incomplete and hence seek concreteness or embodiment in nature. The embodiment of the abstract structures of being in nature is religiously expressed by the doctrine of creation. God the Father is the Creator of the world. In creation the Father moves to fuller reality.

The act of creation, or to put it more accurately in philosophical terms, the concretion or embodiment of the underlying logical structures, gives rise to the second order of reality: the realm of nature. In religious terms this is the kingdom of the Son or the Second Person of the Trinity. The idea of God the Son here signifies not simply Jesus Christ but the whole of the finite, natural world. Just as in the doctrine of the Trinity the Son is eternally begotten by the Father, so the realm of pure being eternally begets the finite world. The natural world for Hegel is viewed as an aspect or part of the total divine life. But this does not mean that Father and Son are identical, or that pure being and nature are the same thing. The begetting of the Son by the Father is a process of self-limitation or kenosis. The Son, a symbol of the finite world of nature, is the opposite of the abstract, infinite world of pure being, the Father. So although there is an underlying unity, there is also real opposition or difference between Father and Son. The antithesis between Father and Son, or the realm of pure being and that of nature, is not final. This opposition is transcended or overcome in the third and highest level of reality: spirit. In religious terms the spirit is called the kingdom of the Spirit, or the Third Person of the Trinity. The way in which this opposition is overcome is expressed in the doctrine of the procession of the Spirit from the Father and Son together. In the classical doctrine of the Trinity the Spirit derives his being from the relation of the Father and the Son. The Father and Son together give rise to the Spirit, which is the bond of union between them. Similarly, the interaction of the two previous levels of reality, pure being and nature, give rise to the new dimension of reality called spirit. Spirit transcends the opposition between pure being and nature. It is the bond of union between these levels of reality, and as such it represents a fuller or higher level of reality than the other two. It contains them, but it also transcends them. In spirit the basic relatedness of all reality, both pure thought and nature, is made evident. In this way world-process reaches full consciousness or understanding of itself. The realm of spirit is necessary for the full reality of all other existence. Similarly, in the doctrine of the Trinity, the full reality of God is dependent on the inter-action of all three Persons: Father, Son, and Holy Spirit.

The rise of spirit is actually the completion of the kenosis-exaltation pattern seen in all reality. The emptying or limita-tion was the transition from the realm of pure being to the realm of nature, or as it is called religiously, the transition from the kingdom of the Father to the kingdom of the Son. The infinite, abstract realm of pure being limited itself to finite, particular existence by being embodied in nature. Now with the rise of full consciousness or spirit in the world-process there has been an exaltation. Spirit presupposes pure being and nature, but it transcends them to a higher level of reality. This is symbolized in the language of the New Testament as the exaltation of the Christ to the new and higher status of " Lord." Because the Christ had accepted limitations and finally death in the " form of a servant " — here symbolic of existence in the realm of na-ture — he has been made " Lord." The preexistence of Christ in the "form of God " is symbolic of the realm of pure being that is a lower level of reality than the realm of spirit. So in the inner development of the world-process, or Absolute, there is a kenosis-exaltation pattern that is presented in the New Testament. In the New Testament this pattern is presented by a *Vorstellung*, a pictorial representation in the form of a quasi-historical myth about the life, death, and resurrection of Jesus. In church dogma this same picture of reality is presented in terms of the doctrine of the Trinity. In philosophical discourse the pattern is pre-sented in the logical idea of the transition from pure being to nature to spirit.

There are some important points in which popular religious thought is misleading. It does not always give a completely accurate picture of the nature of reality through its doctrines.

This is particularly true with the doctrines of creation and reconciliation. In his reinterpretation of them Hegel introduces important changes.

Hegel develops his doctrine of creation out of his basic conviction that world-process consists of the interaction of pure being, nature, and spirit. World-process is threefold with all the parts interdependent. Religiously, this is symbolized when Christians speak of God only as a Trinity. The doctrine of the Trinity states that the members of the Trinity cannot be thought to exist out of relation to one another. Father, Son, and Holy Spirit are so related that the existence of one presupposes the existence of the others. Similarly, each aspect of reality presupposes the other. Just as the relationships between Father, Son, and Holy Spirit are eternal, so the relations between the various aspects of reality are eternal. The eternal quality of these relations is an important point on which the popular religious imagination is easily misled. For example, when talking of the transition from the realm of the Father to the realm of the Son, which is the transition from pure being to nature, the religious mind often misunderstands it as a temporal act. This is what has happened in the doctrine of creation. The coming into existence of the world is pictured as having happened at a certain time. Religion pictures creation as a particular event. Actually it is an eternal process. The Father is always begetting the Son. The abstract structures of pure being are always being embodied in nature in a process of mutual self-limitation.

Religious thinking is also open to a similar misunderstanding in connection with the doctrine of reconciliation, which also unfolds the basic nature of reality. Christianity has made the eternal process of reconciliation between God and man a temporal one. By insisting that reconciliation was accomplished through the events of Jesus' death and resurrection, religion has pictured it as a temporal event with a definite before and after. Jesus' death and resurrection did in fact reveal the divine-human reconciliation. But the source of this reconciliation was far deeper. Reconciliation is grounded in the nature of God himself.

This then is the explication of reconciliation, that God is reconciled with the world, or rather that God has shown Himself to *be* by His very nature reconciled with the world, that what is human is not something alien to His nature, . . . but is a moment in God Himself.[42]

Reconciliation, like creation, is an expression of the basic pattern that characterizes all reality. Kenosis and exaltation is the pattern of the inner life of the Trinity, the creation of the world and the reconciliation of God and man. God is estranged from himself in the finite world. But God in the form of finite existence is also reconciled to himself through the Spirit. Finitude and separation do not have the final word.

The key religious figure through whom this understanding of reconciliation is revealed is Jesus. At first, Jesus was perceived by his followers as a teacher, friend, and martyr. They did not perceive him in the Spirit. Viewed in this way, he was a good and great man. But through his death and resurrection his followers were able to conceive of him spiritually. The tiny community of believers came to the conviction: "God has appeared in the form of Man." "The human is God as immediate and present." This truth is first perceived by Jesus' followers who form the church, the Spiritual Community

It is with the consciousness of the Spiritual Community, which thus makes the transition from man pure and simple to a God-man, and to a certainty of the unity and union of the Divine and human natures that the Church begins.[43]

This perception of the unity of the divine and human is the basic truth in all the Christological affirmations. It is the unique belief of the Christian church. The human life and ultimately the death of Jesus reveal the complete estrangement or self-emptying of the divine into human form. The resurrection and ascension reveal the triumph of the divine Spirit over the conditions of finitude. In this way the eternal unity of the divine and human was made known to the religious mind.

The important point in the Christological affirmations, as in the doctrines of creation and reconciliation, is to perceive their true rational content. The Christological doctrines when viewed religiously picture Christ as having effected in his life, death, and resurrection, the reconciliation between God and man. In reality, Christ reveals the underlying unity of God and man which is eternal. The reconciliation of God and man stems out of the basic nature of reality: finite spirit and Absolute Spirit are ultimately at one. To cast the function of Jesus in this light is not to rob him of his importance. For it was in the church's perception of Jesus' God-manhood that the true relationship between God and man was first made clear. But the idea of God-manhood does not stem from the contingent, historical life of Jesus of Nazareth. It stems from the underlying nature of reality. Jesus revealed this reality, but he did not create it.

The Promise and Peril of Hegelian Theology

Hegel made a vital contribution to any future discussion of Christology or the doctrine of God. He described a doctrine of God that is dynamic. His doctrine envisaged God as being able to accept change and limitation. In fact, finitude is a necessary aspect of the divine life. God is not, as in the classical ontology of church dogma, static, abstract being. Rather, God is conceived in terms of creative process. Here is a conception of God for which the notion of kenosis was neither extraneous nor irrational. Instead, kenosis is the very ground plan of the divine life. Thus there was opened for the first time a way to formulate an intellectually consistent kenotic Christology. By picturing kenosis as an eternal aspect of God, many of the problems inherent in the kenotic Christology could be solved.

The importance of Hegelian doctrine for the formulation of a kenotic Christology had been largely overlooked by the mediating school. Thomasius, for example, had ignored Hegel as an embodiment of " the destructive tendencies of modern thought," largely because of his supposed pantheism. However, there were theologians who had accepted Hegel's philosophy as the basis of their restatement of the Christian faith. Of this group Theodore Liebner (1803–1871) applied Hegel's doctrine to the formulation of a kenotic Christology. His work first appeared in 1849 under the title *Christology or the Christological Unity of Dogmatic Systems.* This was the first volume of a dogmatics that was never completed. Liebner had studied the kenotic Christology of Thomasius and the other theologians of the mediating school. He found much of value in their work. But he had concluded that Thomasius could never arrive at an intellectually consistent kenotic Christology because of the inadequate doctrine of God from which he proceeded. Liebner pointed out the inability of Thomasius to account for the changes in the divine life that a real kenosis involves. This difficulty Liebner believed could be overcome by the use of a Hegelian doctrine of God. His Christology was an attempt to vindicate this claim.

The fragmentary character and often confusing style of Liebner's writing render the interpretation of his Christology difficult. In the main it seems to be dominated by two questions: (1) What makes the incarnation possible? (2) What is the meaning of the historical life of Jesus? Liebner answers this first question by an affirmation of the kenosis. The incarnation is possible because there is a divine self-emptying that allows God to become man. But the kenosis is not a special act of God occurring at the time of Jesus' birth. Rather, kenosis is an eternal quality of God himself. The kenotic surrender of the divine mode of existence and acceptance of humanity are implicit in the immanent life of the Trinity. The eternal kenosis was explained by the subordination of the Son to the Father. The Son derives his being from the Father and is of a lower order than the Father. Even in his preexistent state the Son can be said to derive his being from a self-limitation of the Father. The incarnation is this eternal kenosis being made actual on the plane of history in the person of Jesus of Nazareth. This human life into which the Son enters is not a mode of existence foreign to him. For there is a sense in which the eternal Son already has a side or aspect of his being that can be called eternal manhood. As

Liebner put it, " The Trinitarian Logos already has a side which can be called eternal manhood." [44]

In his preexistent state the Son has not reached full self-consciousness. The consciousness of the Son is lost or hidden in the Father. The Son comes to full reality or complete self-consciousness through his human life as Jesus of Nazareth. This is Liebner's answer to his second question. What is the meaning of the historical life of Jesus? The life of Jesus is a necessary stage in the full development of the Son. The gradual development of Jesus' unique divine-human consciousness during his human life was in reality the gradual unfolding and enrichment of the eternal Son. The full realization Jesus had of his divine nature and mission by the end of his earthly ministry represents not only the growth of a human consciousness; it is God coming to full consciousness or reality. The life of Jesus is a necessary stage in the emergence of God to full reality.

Liebner claimed that in his Christology he had been able to solve the very core problem over which Thomasius had stumbled. Thomasius was left with the problem of what happened to the Trinity if one member of it withdrew for thirty years to become Jesus. Thomasius could not solve the problem of how to relate changes at a particular time in the divine life to the eternal intra-Trinitarian relations. Liebner solved this problem by making kenosis one of the eternal intra-Trinitarian relations. Kenosis is not a happening to which the Trinity must adjust. Kenosis is an eternal quality of Trinitarian life that is expressed at one point in history. The self-limitation of the divine implied in kenosis has always existed in the Trinity because of the subordination of the Son to the Father. Hence, there is no need to explain how a divine limitation could occur to make the life of Jesus possible. Liebner was freed of all the arbitrary juggling of divine attributes by which the mediating school had sought to explain kenosis. He was able to build a Christology of greater intellectual consistency than had his contemporaries. But he had done this through substituting the Hegelian idea of the Absolute for the church doctrine of the Trinity. Although there are many similarities between these two ideas of God, they are far from identical. This was a fact the conservative critics of the Hegelian theology were quick to point out.

As the theological implications of Hegel's philosophy became apparent in the work of the so-called left-wing theologians, there was a ground swell of opposition. Some of this opposition was the shrill outcries of small minds and vested interests appalled at anything new. Yet there were many who spoke out of deep concern and real knowledge. They wondered if Hegel did not threaten to scuttle the ship of Christian faith with his attempts to stop its intellectual leakage. As Hegel's ideas were applied to theology by Liebner, A. E. Biedermann (1819–1895), Philipp K. Marheineke (1780–1846), and others, it became increasingly clear there was an incongruity with certain basic Biblical motifs that could not be overcome. While seeking to give ontological formulation to the basic Biblical faith in the living God through his dynamic conception of deity, Hegel slighted other important aspects of that faith. These difficulties became apparent in his doctrine of creation and in his conception of the historical Jesus.

In his doctrine of creation, Hegel melded two traditional dogmas into one: the doctrine of the Trinity and the doctrine of creation. By doing this, he tended to obliterate the important distinction Christian doctrine has made between God and the world. In Hegel's doctrine of creation, the relation of God to the world is described as the relation of the Father to the Son in the Trinity. The Son is a symbol of nature or the finite order. The Father is the symbol of pure being which is the source of the finite order. In the doctrine of the Trinity the relation of Son to Father is eternal and necessary. The Son is eternally begotten by the Father and always dependent on him. The Father in turn is dependent on the Son, for without a Son he could never be called Father. Hegel used this relationship to characterize the relation of God the Creator, or pure being, to the world of nature. The relation of God to the world is eternal and necessary. God could not reach his full actuality without the world. Not only is the world always dependent on God, but God could never attain his full reality without the world. God and the world coexist as thesis and antithesis. Through their interaction they give rise to the synthesis that is Spirit.

Such a formulation of the doctrine of creation, Hegel's critics declared, was a denial of the aseity, or independence, of God. God in the Hegelian picture is no longer the self-sufficient Creator who by a fiat of will brings the world into existence. Rather, God is dependent upon the world for the completion of his own being. The world is actually an aspect of the divine. God is only half real without the world. So creation is not so much an expression of the sovereign freedom of God as an attempt of God to complete his incompleteness. In his effort to describe the ongoing, dynamic relation of God to the world, Hegel had made God dependent on the world for his full existence. Thus the very divine absoluteness that he was trying to describe and rationally vindicate has been denied by Hegel. Having forsaken the Biblical doctrine of creation, Hegel was betrayed, according to his critics, into a doctrine that bordered on pantheism at worst or a limited God at best.

The other major area of conflict for the Hegelian reinterpretation of doctrine was in Christology. Particularly, the problem was one of the importance of Jesus' earthly existence. Hegel had repeatedly treated the life of Jesus as the supreme revelation to the religious mind of the nature of reality. In Jesus, men saw for the first time that God and man are ultimately one. Yet this revelation was not unique or final. In fact, because of its historical character the revelation in Christ lacked the rational clarity and cogency these same ideas had when derived philosophically. The insights into reality through the life, death, and resurrection of Jesus had their final vindication in philosophy. Jesus is the symbol, the one who points to the underlying realities of life, but he is not the sole key to them.

This aspect of Hegel's thought became glaringly clear in the work of David Friederich Strauss. Strauss brought together in his *Life of Jesus* the Hegelian dialectical scheme with the science of Biblical criticism. He explained the growth of the New Testament picture of Jesus as the development of a myth. The main function of this myth is to set forth the conception that God and man are ultimately one.

When mankind is once sufficiently developed to have as its religion the truth that God is man and man of divine race, this truth, since religion is the form assumed by truth for the ordinary mind, must be shown in a manner comprehensible by all as a sensible certainty, i.e., a human individual must arise who is regarded as the present God.[45]

But the life of this "human individual" is not necessarily a historical demonstration of God-manhood through miracles or other supernatural events. His God-manhood is not vindicated by historical proofs. Rather, Jesus is the occasion for the development of a myth that teaches the underlying unity of God and man. The historicity of Jesus as had always been insisted upon by orthodox Christianity had now been pushed completely into the background. The origins of Christianity, for Strauss, were not so much in the life of a person as in a group of ideas. The truth of these ideas is not found in their historical illustration but in their innate philosophical cogency. Before the higher conception of truth, the historical illustration shrinks in importance to the disappearing point.

As a latter-day critic of Hegelianism said of Strauss's *Life of Jesus:* " It disposed for good and all of the hallucination that Christian belief and consistent Hegelianism are two forms of the same thing." [46] To the conservative critics of Hegel, the work of Strauss tended to verify their worst suspicions. Often they condemned Hegel for what Strauss said without troubling to see whether they were saying the same thing. In many points they were not in agreement. But the controversy over Strauss did set in clear perspective the difficulties of using Hegel's ontology as the basis of interpreting the radically historical religion of the Bible. Hegel could not give to the particular embodiment of truth in Jesus the ultimacy claimed for it in Christian faith. Because all historical reality is in process, no moment in it can be absolute. Absoluteness is found only in the structures that shape history. And these underlying rational structures can only be certainly known philosophically. History may illustrate world-process, but no particular moment in history can be the final key to world-process.

Because of these difficulties, in part, and because of the changing fashions in theological thinking, Hegel's rich and suggestive treatment of the kenosis motif played little part in the Christological developments of the late nineteenth century. The mediating school remained hostile or wary of Hegel's treatment of kenosis. The Hegelians gave increasingly scant attention to the kenotic Christology. Their attention was turned elsewhere. By the time the last edition of Thomasius' treatment of the kenosis theory appeared in 1886 the idea had passed from the center of theological attention on the Continent. The next chapter in the unfolding history of the kenosis motif was to be written in the English-speaking world.

CHAPTER VII

Kenosis and the Moralizing of Dogma

KENOSIS DOCTRINE IN THE ENGLISH-SPEAKING WORLD

The Shift of Scene

With the waning of interest among the Continental theologians, concern with kenotic Christology did not cease. Rather, the center of attention shifted to the English-speaking world, where kenosis doctrine remained important until well into this century. The theological concerns that had brought modern kenotic Christology into existence in Germany were not keenly felt among English-speaking theologians until the latter part of the nineteenth century. The growing traffic of theological ideas from the German schools during the last half of the century pressed upon the often reluctant mind of English Christianity the necessity for rethinking doctrine in the light of critico-historical scholarship. Historical scholarship was making increasingly clear the reality of Jesus' humanity. And theologians were seeking a convincing way to relate this new picture of Jesus' humanity to the orthodox doctrine of his divinity. To these theologians, as to Thomasius and his associates in the previous generation, the kenotic motif appeared to be the most convincing alternative at hand.

The kenotic Christologies of the English-speaking theologians were dependent on the work of their Continental predecessors, but they were not simply copies. The moderating change, which theological ideas have often undergone in their movement across the English Channel, was evident in the new forms of kenosis doctrine that appeared in the English-speaking world. Specifically, two concerns served to give the new kenotic Christologies their unique character. First, there was a reserve among the English theologians about the use of speculative reason in interpreting the meaning of kenosis. The English theologians preferred to remain mute on questions about kenosis and the inner life of the Trinity. They did not share the confidence of the previous generation of Continental theologians in giving rational solutions to all the problems posed by kenosis. As P. T. Forsyth put it: "We cannot form any scientific conception of the precise process by which a complete and eternal being could enter on a process of becoming, how Godhead could accept growth, how a divine consciousness could reduce its own consciousness by volition." [47] This reserve served the English theologians well, delivering them from the more bizarre and arbitrary aspects of kenosis doctrine found among the Germans. Kenosis was not for them a principle of intelligibility to explain every aspect of the divine life as it had been for the Germans. Kenosis illumined part of the mystery of incarnation, but it does not make the mystery disappear.

The second distinctive feature of the kenotic Christologies among the English is their close relation to empirical study of the Bible. The Continental theologians had assuredly been concerned to root their doctrine in Scripture. But the kenotic motif had quickly been abstracted from the Bible to be interpreted in essentially philosophical and psychological ways. English theology sought to ground its work in specific studies of the Gospels and epistles. As the English writers saw the kenotic Christology, it was a Biblical doctrine used to integrate the pictures of Jesus found in the Gospels. The basic authority of the doctrine was derived from its place in Scripture, rather than from its helpfulness in solving certain theological problems. Hence, kenosis doctrine was often retained despite the speculative problems that so clearly attend it. As Forsyth remarked, "The science of it can wait; the religion of it cannot." [48] This impatience with speculative difficulties and devotion to Biblical grounding gave to kenosis doctrine in the

English-speaking world its distinctive flavor.

The kenotic Christologies of the Germans were first introduced to the English scene by A. B. Bruce in his Cunningham Lectures, *The Humiliation of Christ*, 1876. The presentation was sympathetic, but his final word was one of suspended judgment rather than uncritical support. The kenosis theme was also investigated by such Biblical scholars as T. K. Cheyne and Bishop J. B. Lightfoot. But the wave of popular interest in kenosis doctrine awaited an essay by Charles Gore in his epoch-making book, *Lux Mundi*, 1889. Actually, Gore mentioned the kenosis ideas only as an aside in an essay dealing with the inspiration of Scripture.[49] In the course of his essay, Gore demonstrated that Jesus' knowledge was limited. Specifically, Jesus was unaware of historical inaccuracies in the Old Testament. Jesus accepted the commonly held views on the Old Testament of a first-century Jew. Gore suggested that such limitation is not inconsistent with Christ's divinity. During his earthly ministry Christ had accepted a limitation upon his divine omniscience. As a true human being, Jesus shared human limitations in knowledge. Gore was immediately attacked as a Nestorian by the defenders of orthodoxy because, they argued, any limitation of knowledge would mean a limitation of divinity. Gore had challenged the assumption long made that the omniscience of the divine nature would prevent any limitation of knowledge in Jesus. To make good on this challenge Gore set about expanding and vindicating a doctrine of divine self-limitation in Christ. This he did in a number of works reaching fullest presentation in *Dissertations on Subjects Connected with the Incarnation*, 1895.

Gore based his work on a careful exegesis of Scripture and detailed studies of the fathers. He acknowledged the work of the Continental theologians, finding the best treatment of the kenosis theme in Bishop Martensen of Denmark. With Martensen, Gore maintained that the self-emptying of the Logos was partial. The Logos still retained his divine nature. The divine glory and full functioning of the divine attributes were

surrendered in the incarnation so that Jesus was a truly human
being. But such a surrender did not mean that the Logos had
abdicated his world-ruling function. The self-emptying of the
Logos affected only part of its being, namely, that part involved in the person of Jesus. In all other respects the Logos
continues its full divine activity. The limitation of the Logos
in Jesus is simply to assure the reality of his human consciousness. The Logos leads a dual life as unlimited World-Ruler
and as limited in a human personality. While not unaware of
the theological problems involved in this affirmation of a dual
life for the Logos, Gore did not feel the necessity for present-
ing a fully rational picture of the divine self-emptying. He was
content to use the kenotic motif to explain Jesus' human consciousness, while making no attempt to repair the incongruity
this poses for the doctrine of the Trinity. The kenotic motif
is applied in only one sector of the Christological problem. The
broader concerns for the doctrine of God fell outside the scope
of his immediate interest. They were to remain wrapped in
mystery.

Gore's approach to the kenotic motif was characteristic of
the theologians of the English-speaking world. Principal Fairbairn, of Mansfield College, H. R. Mackintosh, of Edinburgh,
and the Anglicans, Frank Weston and E. H. Gifford, all ex-
pounded the kenotic theme in their Christologies with learning
and insight. In fact, interest in the kenosis became something
of a fad, leaving untold references to it throughout the theological literature of the time. Most of these treatments fall into
a pattern. Generally these writers followed the lead of the
more conservative Continental theologians, such as Thomasius
or Martensen, rather than the bolder and more speculative
writers, such as Liebner and Ebrard. They were all anxious to
retain the full divinity of Christ and his place in the Trinity
as the World-Ruler. They were also committed to the new
understanding of Jesus' fully human consciousness emerging
from the critical study of the New Testament. But these men
despaired of propounding a systematic and consistent doctrine

of kenotic Christology. They did not advance the understanding of kenosis. Rather, they settled for a limited and unsystematic application of the kenotic motif to the problem of Jesus' consciousness. They were not unaware of the need for full and systematic treatment of the subject. They simply recognized the inability of existing patterns of thought to produce a fully integrated picture of the divine self-emptying.

The Christology of P. T. Forsyth

The major step toward reconstruction of kenosis doctrine among the English writers was taken by the Congregational preacher and theologian Peter Taylor Forsyth (1848–1923). He gave an extensive treatment of the kenosis theme in *The Person and Place of Jesus Christ* and in numerous essays. The Christology that emerges from his extensive writings is more often fragmentary and suggestive than systematic. This is in part due to his literary style, which bears the impress of homiletical language that often implies more than it actually states. His thought often proceeds by means of simile, metaphor, personal analogies, and stories. But the difficulties to be faced in garnering a clear picture of Forsyth's Christology spring also in part from his struggles with a new theological methodology. Forsyth's thought about the kenotic Christology was part of his total program for rethinking Christian doctrine called " the moralizing of dogma." He was trying to find new and more adequate categories for theological reflection. Although the results of this effort were not always clear and consistent, they do provide provocative insight on basic problems. In order to evaluate properly Forsyth's Christology, it is first necessary to understand his theological method or program for " moralizing dogma."

The moralizing of dogma is essentially an attempt to find new and more adequate forms of theological language. Forsyth believed theological thought was often stymied by its excessive use of abstract ontological terms. He believed Christian doctrine had to be restated in a language more congenial to its basic nature. For him this meant the restatement of Christianity in personalistic and moral terms. The basic key for understanding Christian doctrine is found in the unique moral experience of forgiveness through Jesus Christ. Christian faith can only be comprehended in terms of what it is — a personal moral experience based on Christ. Speculative philosophical language is incapable of setting forth Christian faith by its very nature. It is abstract and impersonal. Ontological thought is characterized by logical necessity rather than moral choice. Only as Christian faith is thought about in personalistic and moral terms can its uniqueness be set forth.

Forsyth believed this restatement of Christian faith was a necessity for two reasons. First, his concern in moralizing dogma was apologetic. He wanted to give a cogent restatement of Christianity to a generation whose thought had been shaped by personalism in philosophy and by a deepened concern for ethics in religion. If Christian faith was to speak to modern man, it must speak in terms of personal ethical experience, not in terms of speculative dogma. Second, his concern was kerygmatic as well as apologetic. Forsyth was deeply concerned with bringing theology into closer conformity with its sources in Scripture. He was convinced that theological thought had become increasingly estranged from the basic modes of thought found in the Bible. In response to this problem, the moralizing of dogma was to be a restatement of Christianity in the personal and moral terms congenial to its sources.

In the light of the moralizing of dogma, the proper key to understanding Christ is not speculation about his two natures. Rather, it is the personal, moral experience of forgiveness of sins through him. Moral certainty rather than intellectual illumination is the basic hallmark of Christian faith. For this reason, Christianity must proceed from this basic moral experience in the statement of its Christology. It is important to note here that such a moralizing of dogma does not mean the reduction of Christology to a series of statements about the historical Jesus as a moral teacher. Forsyth's conception of moral experience is far more inclusive than this. Instead, Christology is to be the investigation of the presuppositions of the moral experience of forgiveness through Christ.

> We are to think about Christ whatever is required to explain the most certain thing in the soul's experience — namely, that he has given it the new life of God and mercy, and saved it from the old life of guilt, self and world.[50]

By means of what Forsyth terms "inspired, divinely guided inference," Christian faith gradually gave voice in the New Testament to three basic affirmations about Christ. They are the affirmations of the preexistence of Christ, the kenosis or self-emptying of Christ, and the plerosis or self-fulfillment of Christ. These affirmations are not so much dogmatic propositions as ideas used to explain the depth and reality of the Christian experience of forgiveness. These affirmations are inferences made on the basis of Christian experience about how Christ is related to God and to man.

Within such a framework what is the meaning of the preexistence of Christ? The doctrine of preexistence explains the scope of the Christian experience of salvation. The doctrine is "to give range to the soul's greatness by displaying the vast postulates of its redemption." The salvation offered through Christ is a cosmic salvation of which my personal faith is but a tiny fragment. Christ's saving work embraces the whole creation and can only be understood as the work of God himself. The salvation he offers is nothing else but a new creation. Such a salvation could never have been brought about by human action, even the action of a perfectly good man. Hence, the only way in which such a salvation can be understood is if there is a unity between the Creator and the Savior. It is this unity that is asserted in the doctrine of the preexistence of Christ.

> We are driven by the real existence of an Eternal Father and our experience of his grace, to demand the existence of an equally eternal Son — both being equally personal and divine.[51]

Preexistence explains the scope of the Christian experience of forgiveness as a forgiveness granted by God himself working through a Son with whom he is in perfect and eternal unity.

Yet the very way in which the doctrine of preexistence is formulated poses a problem. For although Christian faith sees the depth and reality of Christ's relationship to the Father, it also sees another fact. Christ is a fully human being. So Christian faith is not content to stop with the affirmation of preexistence. The inner logic of faith drives it onward to the next Christological affirmation, the doctrine of the divine kenosis. The attempt to relate Christ's preexistence to his true humanity leads inevitably to a consideration of his act of self-emptying.

In interpreting the divine self-emptying, Forsyth focuses attention primarily on the problem of the divine and human consciousness of Christ. The basic question is, How can an infinite consciousness be thought of as reducing itself to a finite one? More precisely, Forsyth believed the problem to be how the divine consciousness of the eternal Son can limit itself to a finite form and still retain continuity with its preincarnate form. Any answer to this question must guard against two extremes. It must reject the error of classical orthodoxy in conceiving kenosis as a mere veiling of the divine consciousness and activity. It must also avoid the extreme of modernism, as seen in Frederic Godet, which teaches that kenosis is the obliteration of the divine consciousness.[52] Forsyth sees kenosis as implying both a limitation and a continuity of the divine consciousness in the man Jesus. He tries to explain this idea by a number of analogies from human experience. The most apt of these is the story of a university student who shows clear genius in philosophy. He is the only son in a large family. At a critical point in his family's business affairs his father dies. It is his duty to forsake his beloved studies to return home to carry on the business and support the rest of his family. He accepts his duty and leaves the realm of thought and life so dear to him to enter one that is alien and remote. In time he comes to forget the delights of the world of thought and loses his skills in it. He must be content to be at best a learned amateur. He has accepted the moral call into the realm of business life in which he is now immersed, able only to long for a life he forsook. He has voluntarily accepted a contraction of his consciousness in response to a higher moral call.

Such an analogy is naturally not fully applicable to Christ. But it does illumine two basic aspects of the divine self-emptying in Christ. First, kenosis implies a voluntary contraction of consciousness in response to a higher moral call. Self-emptying was Christ's free moral response to the situation posed by human sinfulness. The preexistent Christ accepted limitation of his divine consciousness and activity in order to fulfill the human need for divine forgiveness. The Christ could bring this forgiveness. But he could bring it only as a man. Hence, he was under a moral demand to accept self-limitation into a human life. He freely accepted this moral call and so brought about the salvation of the world. Second, the story describes a contraction of consciousness in which a thread of continuity remains. The self-emptying of Christ means primarily a contraction or concentration of the full divine consciousness of the preexistent state. It was a retraction so complete that Christ could become the victim of human sin and death. Yet even in this retracted state there was still continuity between the preincarnate and the incarnate Christ. Incarnation does not mean an obliteration of the divine but its concentration into a highly limited form. In the story the philosophy student retained a limited knowledge and a continued interest in the studies that had once taken all his time and energy. The link with the period of full philosophical consciousness was not broken although now highly attenuated. In the same way the divine consciousness of the Christ is no longer present in its fullness. Rather, it remains as the longing of Jesus for the heavenly realm and his desire to serve the Father. The divine consciousness that had once been at the full remained as a small but real reminder of its former state.

Having explained the divine self-emptying in this way, Forsyth is faced by a perennial problem for kenotic Christologies. In what sense can the incarnate Christ be thought of as uniquely and fully divine? Having so vigorously asserted the limitations of God in Christ, what then is to be said of the reality of God in Christ? In answering this question, Forsyth makes a subtle combination of the teachings of Ebrard and Thomasius. First, in agreement with Ebrard, Forsyth says kenosis is not accomplished by the renunciation of certain attributes like omniscience, etc. The divine life and action is unitary and cannot be split into groups of attributes. For this reason the term self-emptying is perhaps misleading. The more apt term to explain kenosis would be self-reduction or self-retraction. The divine attributes enter a new mode of being in which they are retracted from full actuality to potentiality. They do not cease thereby to exist. They are only concentrated and come to expression in different form. In the incarnate Christ the divine attributes no longer function in the physical realm but in the moral. And the mode of their activity grows and expands with the development of Jesus' personality. Omniscience is transformed from the intuitive and simultaneous knowledge of all things to the discursive and successive knowledge common to men. The divine omnipotence is not arbitrary power. It is the implementation of the Father's will of holy love. Omnipotence becomes the freedom to fulfill the demands of God's love. This freedom is most fully expressed in God's accepting the limitation of creating other free beings and finally in entering the confines of human life himself. "The freedom that limits itself to create freedom is true omnipotence, as the love that can humble itself to save is truly almighty."[53]

Secondly, the retraction of the divine life in Christ does not vitiate his divinity because the acceptance of limitation is an expression of power, not a defect. Forsyth follows Thomasius' basic affirmation about kenosis: "Self-limitation is self-determination." Forsyth expresses this in terms of the divine freedom: "The freedom that accepts limits itself to create freedom is true omnipotence." God's highest power is his ability to accept the limitation of a human life and yet not become unlike himself. If this limitation could not be accepted, then there would indeed be a limit on God's power, namely, the necessity of avoiding limitation. " If he could not become incarnate His infinitude would be partial and limited. . . . It would be limited by human nature in the sense of not being able to enter it." [54] In this light, the act of kenosis itself becomes the highest expression of Christ's divinity. His ability to accept freely and fully the limitations of human life is the evidence of his divinity.

Forsyth sees yet another difficulty besetting his interpretation of kenosis. Does the retraction of the divine consciousness necessary for Christ to be a true man make it possible for him to sin? In asking this question, Forsyth is trying to determine negatively the limits to be set to the retraction of the divine consciousness in Jesus. He answers that the limit set for retraction of the divine consciousness is Christ's inability to sin. The divine consciousness is not retracted to such a point as to allow Christ to become a sinner. But such a position brings into question the reality of Christ's human personality. Is not one of the marks of humanity its freedom to sin? To deny at least this possibility would be to deny the reality of Jesus' humanity. Forsyth understands the cogency of such arguments and tries to deal with them. He deals with these objections through an investigation of just what is essential to true humanity.

Sin and guilt as such do not belong to true humanity, although they are very much a part of empirical humanity. The characteristic of man is not sin but the ability to be tempted by sin. Temptation itself is not sin. It is, rather, the condition of moral freedom. In this ability to be tempted Christ shared fully. "He could be tempted because he loved; he could not sin because he loved so deeply." [55] Yet even to this position cannot objection be taken? For to say Christ could not sin would be to rob his experience of temptation of any reality. This would make of Christ's struggles with temptation a sham battle. But this is not the case. Christ's moral struggles were real because his limited knowledge meant he did not know the outcome in advance. His inability to sin remained unknown to him until his life's end. Each struggle was real as far as it was known to his conscious mind. Yet even such reflections on the sinlessness of Christ are never fully adequate to explain his moral and spiritual struggles. The exact nature of what transpired, Forsyth concedes, remains locked in the secret of his personality. Such theories as we have are but crude approximations.

So it was that God entered fully upon our common life by an act of self-retraction. Christ was a true man, a normal man, who was not necessarily a brilliant man. His knowledge was limited, and its growth followed a normal human development. But to consider Christ in terms of this kenosis alone is only part of the picture. Amid the moral crises and victories of his earthly life there was growing to full actuality the divine consciousness that had been retracted. In the life of Christ culminating in the cross and its victory there was coming to Christ the power over heaven and earth given him by the Father.

In finding the sheep that were lost he gradually finds the self, the mode of self, the consciousness he had renounced. . . . The diminuendo of the kenosis went on parallel with the crescendo of a vaster plerosis.[56]

The Christology that stops with kenosis alone is inevitably lopsided. For the Christian experience on which Christology is based has within it more than knowledge of God who humbled himself to enter the human realm. Christian experience reveals also God as he entered the trials of this life and triumphed over them. The incarnation is not simply the renunciation of the divine. There is also in it growth, achievement, and exaltation that found its culmination in the resurrection and return to glory. The person of Christ is to be considered from a twofold point of view. It is not only a matter of kenosis but also of a subsequent plerosis or self-fulfillment. Plerosis is not only the exaltation of the resurrection-ascension at the end of Jesus' earthly ministry. The plerosis is a basic characteristic of his whole life. Each moral and spiritual victory won by Christ in his human life marked a step in this process of divine growth or self-fulfillment. Considered in its fullness, the incarnation involves the condescending movement of God to man — kenosis — and the ascending movement of man to God — plerosis. It is these two movements which determine the person of Christ.

This kenosis-plerosis theme becomes for Forsyth the basis for reconstruction of the classical doctrine of the two natures in terms of a new metaphysic, " a metaphysic of faith." The divine and human in Christ are no longer to be considered in terms of being and nature. The doctrine of Christ is to be restated in terms of will, ethics, and personality. The central interest in the classical statements about the person of Christ was the assertion of his deity as the source of our salvation. This must be retained. But the ontology of these creeds must be replaced because it is ultimately incapable of expressing the meaning of Christ. The Christological statements of orthodoxy used abstract categories of being. An adequate Christology for today must use the categories of personal life and morality. Such a modern Christology would seek to describe Christ in terms of the personal movements of kenosis and plerosis.

Having come to this crucial and very promising point in his Christology, Forsyth becomes increasingly enigmatic. This much is clear: he wishes to describe Christ in dynamic terms. The personality of Christ is constituted by a twofold activity: the movement of God to men and the movement of men to God. The interplay of these two movements can be seen in the whole movement of human history and spirituality.

On the one hand we have an initiative, creative, productive action, clear and sure on the part of eternal and absolute God; on the other, we have the seeking, receptive, appropriative action of groping, erring, growing men.[57]

In Christ this whole drama is compassed in a single person. He is the embodiment of God's search for man and man's search for God. The person of Christ does not result from the meeting of two static natures but from the interplay of two personal activities. The person of Christ emerges from what Forsyth calls the "mutual involution" of these two movements. The great question that Forsyth leaves unanswered is what he means by the "mutual involution" of the movement of God to man and man to God. In what sense does the integration of two personal actions give rise to another person?

Negatively, it is clear what Forsyth is rejecting. He wishes to banish once and for all static ontologies from Christological thinking. Incarnation is a personal act of God and man. He also wants to avoid the one-sidedness of those kenotic Christologies that see incarnation only as a limitation of the divine. Incarnation represents a fulfillment of man as much as a limitation of God. Positively, the picture is not so clear. Forsyth does assume an underlying unity between God and man. "Man is indeed incomparable with God, but incompatible he is not." [58] The common quality that God and man share is that both are moral beings. Man is only potentially moral, assuming his true moral character only through forgiveness. God is absolutely moral. Because God and man share this common moral quality, they can be united. They can be united through a mutual action of will. The wills can become one through being fixed on a common moral objective. In the case of Christ this common moral objective is human redemption. The divine-human union in Christ is the confluence of two wills centered on the task of redeeming mankind. This union of wills provides the basis of Jesus' personality. This is the "mutual involution" which shapes the being of Christ.

Forsyth's solution of the Christological question is in many ways reminiscent of that of Nestorius and the Antiochian school in the ancient church. But since it lacks completeness, any pat labeling of it is bound to be misleading. Any judgment of this Christology must be tempered by the realization of the many questions it leaves unanswered. This is a realization which Forsyth himself always had. He closes his Christology with a bold acknowledgment of its limitations. "We cannot see for the glory of that light, and what we do see is beyond man to utter." [59] Knowledge of Christ lies ultimately in the saving experience and worship of Christ in light of his full glory. All human speech is finally silenced before the reality of humanity's Savior.

The Possibility of a Kenotic Christology

The English-speaking theologians of the late nineteenth and early twentieth centuries made a contribution toward understanding kenosis that was both negative and positive. Negatively, their work marked the end of the relation between the mediating tradition in theology and the kenosis doctrine in Christology. Throughout the nineteenth century many of the mediating theologians in Germany and the English-speaking world had tried to preserve some form of the orthodox doctrine of Christ in the modern world by use of the kenotic motif. But the outcome was always the same. While they used kenosis to save part of the house of orthodoxy, another part always seemed to be undermined. While the kenotic motif was being used to solve the problem of Jesus' human consciousness, it created insolvable problems for the doctrine of the Trinity. While showing how Christ was human, the kenotic Christologies were unable to show how he was divine. The English theologians eschewed the solution of these difficulties. They simply settled for taking their problems one at a time. Having solved the problem of Jesus' human consciousness, they left the doctrine of the Trinity wrapped in mystery. Forsyth probably went farther than any of them in dealing with the kenosis doctrine in a complete manner. But as has been seen, most of the irksome problems remained unsolved for him.

The systematic incompleteness of the English kenotic Christologies did preserve them from the more bizarre speculation of the Germans about the inner life of the Trinity. This reserve tempted a latter-day English writer on Christology to indulge in a little theological chauvinism. J. S. Lawton commented, " Hence we shall expect to find the kenotic theory free from all excesses and crudities when presented by the English writers of our period." [60] But avoiding problems is not finally the best way of solving them, so it is not surprising that widespread criticism of the kenotic Christologies arose among the English theologians themselves. This critique was given classic form by William Temple in his *Christus Veritas*, 1924.

But the difficulties are intolerable. What was happening to the rest of the universe during the period of our Lord's earthly life? To say that the Infant Jesus was from His cradle exercising providential care over it all is certainly monstrous; but to deny this, and yet say the Creative Word was so self-emptied as to have no being except in the Infant Jesus, is to assert that for a certain period of history the world was let loose from the control of the Creative Word, and "apart from Him" very nearly everything happened that happened at all during the thirty-odd years, both on this planet and throughout the immensities of space. [61]

On the ground chosen by the mediating theologians for constructing their kenotic Christologies the question posed by Temple was as unavoidable as unanswerable. In this realization many turned to find new approaches to a modern statement of the church's confession of its Lord.

Despite this impasse, some theologians and New Testament scholars have continued to write and think in the older kenotic tradition of the English mediating school. As recently as 1938, Dr. J. M. Creed wrote that despite its current lack of favor the majority of those who still had a Christology that they would state and defend were still kenoticists. In the post World War II period such British New Testament scholars as Vincent Taylor have again demonstrated that some form of kenotic doctrine is an inevitable part of any Christology that claims to be rooted in the New Testament. Yet in these affirmations of kenotic Christology, as deeply felt and important as they may be, there is little promise of the renewal of a full-blown kenotic theory. Such a Christology remains for these theologians a wistful hope rather than a viable reality. For there are no grounds for believing that some greater, and as yet unknown, measure of theological ingenuity can solve the problems facing the kenotic Christology as understood within the mediating tradition. The future of the kenotic motif lies in some other direction.

The work of the English-speaking theologians did more than simply illumine the limitations of the kenotic Christologies. There was in their work a positive contribution that is seen most clearly in Forsyth. This was his attempt to find fresh categories of thought appropriate to the kenotic motif. His search for new thought forms for use in the doctrines of God and Christ pointed to new and constructive possibilities. Forsyth's genius lies in his seeing more clearly than his contemporaries the real source of the impasse in the kenotic theories. He saw the problems were the result of inadequate and inappropriate categories of interpretation. Despite many concerted efforts at modification, the basic pattern of thought about God and Christ among the mediating theologians was still dominated by the Trinitarian doctrine of classical orthodoxy. Within such patterns of thought, Forsyth realized, the divine self-emptying could never be properly comprehended. Kenosis implied changes in the divine life that could never be understood within the traditional doctrine of God. The kenotic motif could not be used to repair this or that part of the sagging house of orthodoxy. It had to become the basis of a total rebuilding job. This was a realization which most of Forsyth's contemporaries did not share. The innate conservatism of the mediating theologians kept them from seeing the far-reaching implications of the kenotic motif. Yet this was Forsyth's insight which he left for future students of the motif to ponder.

The limitation in Forsyth's work lies in his inability to do more than intimate the line this rebuilding of doctrine must take. Having caught a vision of the " promised land," he was not able to cross over and take possession of it. His program for the " moralizing of dogma " remained incomplete. His attempt at a " metaphysic of faith " based on personalistic and moral categories was only an interesting possibility. It did not become a full actuality. So the legacy of the English-speaking interpreters of the kenotic motif remains a problem and a promise. The problem was that of the failure of the kenotic theory to become the touchstone for building a modern Christology. The promise was the possibility of new ways of thought that could more fully comprehend the mystery of the divine self-emptying.

A Historical Addendum on Roman Catholic and Orthodox Christology

At this point many may well ask if there have not been some important omissions in this work. For since the title claims to deal with the kenotic motif throughout church history, proper attention must be given to Roman Catholic and Orthodox thought. The last mention of the Catholic traditions was in the section on patristic and medieval thought. Since that period, attention has been focused exclusively on Protestantism. Is such an exclusion justified? What has been the role of the kenosis motif in the churches of the Catholic tradition both Eastern and Western? These questions must be answered before the elaboration of the kenotic motif in contemporary theology is discussed. For it is evident that kenosis did not somehow become a motif of Protestant Christianity exclusively. It is a motif far too basic and important to become the preserve of any single tradition or group.

The place of the kenotic motif in Roman Catholic Christology was established at the time of the Arian controversy. Following the work of Victorinus and Athanasius, the motif was assimilated into the doctrine of the two natures of Christ. The pattern of this assimilation, as we have seen, is clear. The ambiguous references to the preexistent nature of Christ in the New Testament were all interpreted as referring to the Logos who is coequal and coeternal with the Father. All thought of a subordination in the preexistent state was rejected. And all thought of exaltation to a higher divine status in the ascension was similarly rejected. The actual self-emptying by which the incarnation was made possible was the veiling of the fully divine nature in human flesh. In this pattern of interpretation, all the

New Testament references to the divine limitation in Christ were assimilated into the emerging orthodoxy of Athanasius. The expression " the form of God " from the Philippian hymn was understood as being the fully divine Second Person of the Trinity. The self-emptying was his acceptance of a human body. Once this pattern was set, there were no further developments of the kenotic motif in the formal Christology of Roman Catholicism. Rather, this pattern of thought has been repeated almost without variation from that day to this. The post-Nicene fathers, the theologians of the Middle Ages, and the controversialists of the Counter-Reformation all spoke with one voice on the question of kenosis. Thomas Aquinas, in his *Commentary on the Epistles of Paul*, concluded that anyone who followed another exegesis of the Philippian passage than that of the anti-Arian fathers either did not understand Paul or was a heretic.

Little attention was given to the question of kenosis in modern Roman Catholic thought save for some slighting references to the work of Protestant exegetes during the nineteenth century. The exception to this was a detailed study of the history of the exegesis of Phil. 2:6-8 by Heinrich Schumacher, a German scholar at the Papal Institute of Biblical Studies, in 1914.[62] But the outcome of the study was not a reopening of the question of kenosis. Rather, Schumacher concluded that the unanimity of testimony from linguistic study and the teaching of the great exegetes of the church foreclosed such a possibility. In fact, he was so convinced that the question had been settled once for all he was at a loss to understand the prodigious amounts of scholarly energy Protestants had poured upon it. He finally concluded that such interest was more a witness to the vagaries of Protestantism than to the difficulties in understanding the passage in Philippians. Other Roman Catholic commentators were less charitable in their estimates of the modern kenotic Christologies. In a review of Gess's Christology, one writer quipped that the only emptying he saw in the kenotic theories was an emptying of the understanding of those who held them, while another reviewer said Protestant speculations about kenosis had led them to absurdity. No matter how valid criticisms of many of the kenotic Christologies may be, such attitudes bespeak little understanding of the issues that gave rise to them.

The rigidity of modern Roman Catholicism on the question of kenotic Christology is witness to the rigidity of post-Tridentine Roman Catholic theology in Christology and the doctrine of God. The major factor that exercised the mind of Protestantism in this period — the critico-historical picture of Jesus as a human being — was not a primary causative factor in Roman Catholic theology at that time. And the possibility of recasting the doctrine of God in the light of idealistic or personalistic philosophy was excluded, not only by long-standing dogmatic definitions, but also by the reassertion of Thomistic thought as normative for all theology by Leo XIII. There was within formal Roman Catholic theology neither the stimulus nor the opportunity for the vigorous doctrinal development that marked Protestant Christology in this period.

It would be a mistake, however, to believe the kenotic motif was silent within Roman Catholic piety and preaching despite its static place in theology. The devotion to the Sacred Heart of Jesus, which came to major prominence in the eighteenth century, expresses elements of the kenotic motif. It represents the recovery of the importance of Jesus' humanity for faith within the piety of Roman Catholicism. This devotion is worship centered on the human love of Jesus as symbolized by his heart. The central symbol of devotion is the wounded heart of Jesus — a reminder of his suffering love. The focus of piety is in the moral and emotional life of Jesus. It calls attention to the humanity of Jesus and the fact that he was the victim of suffering and death. Christ is pictured as experiencing the very human emotion of sorrow because his love for mankind has gone unrequited. He longs for the response of love from men in answer to his love for them. The emphasis of the Sacred Heart cult is on Christ as a suffering, dying man, rather

than as triumphant Judge and Ruler. He is viewed in his humiliation rather than his exaltation. From this standpoint the
Sacred Heart devotion can be said to be a reaffirmation of
Christ in his Servant form. It is the Christ who has freely
emptied himself to take up human life with its suffering and
death who is the central figure. And it is through this Christ
who has entered the humble state of man that the believer can
receive the special graces to bear his own humanity. It is the
humility of Christ that allows the believer to know him and
receive salvation through him.

Although the picture of Christ in the Sacred Heart devotion
is kenotic in character, this is not to say that it ever became
the basis of a formal Christological doctrine as such. The dev-
otees of the Sacred Heart devotion adhered fully to the creedal
definitions of their church. It is, rather, that in their devotions
and preaching, the motif of the divine self-limitation in Christ
and his consequent human limitations and suffering plays a decisive role. In this regard the Sacred Heart devotion is very
similar to the kenotic themes found in the Pietism of Zinzendorf with its meditations on the wounds of Christ. Both the
Protestant Pietists and the Sacred Heart cult maintained formal
allegiance to creedal orthodoxy in their Christology. But there
is in their worship and preaching a picture of Christ that is
strongly kenotic. In both these forms of piety the access of the
believer to Christ is through the humanity of Christ. It is the
Christ who has been made one with us in every way, even
to death, who is the key to salvation.

One of the most striking and eloquent expressions of the
kenotic motif within Roman Catholicism is in the preaching
of John Henry Newman (1801–1890). Newman, through his
combination of theological acumen and literary style, brought
the divine self-emptying to focus in an Epiphany sermon,
" Omnipotence in Bonds," 1857. The major contrast on which
the sermon is based is between the omnipotence that rightfully
belongs to Christ and the bondage that he freely accepted in
becoming incarnate. The Christ has freely accepted in every

stage of his earthly life a bondage that had its start when his omnipotence was imprisoned in the womb of the Virgin Mary. This, he says, is " the commencement of the wonderful captivity of the Infinite God." His infancy marked the acceptance of new forms of bondage, subjection to his parents' authority, rejection by his people, and finally the suffering of his passion and death. But this bondage did not cease with his resurrection and ascension. The Infinite God is still in bonds as his very body and blood are found upon the altar.

He took bread, and blessed, and made it His Body; He took wine, and gave thanks, and made it His Blood; and He gave His priests the power to do what He had done. Henceforth, He is in the hands of sinners once more. Frail, ignorant, sinful man, by the sacredotal power given to him, compels the presence of the Highest; he lays Him up in a small tabernacle; he dispenses Him to a sinful people.[63]

The Sacrament on the altar is a continuation of the self-limitation of the earthly ministry. Kenosis is an abiding quality of Christ. It is that quality which brings us most closely into relation with Christ. His humble acceptance of limitation compels an answering humility in all who would be his followers.

Near the end of his sermon, Newman reflects on the relation between the omnipotence and the humility of Christ in a manner recalling Thomasius and the Protestant interpreters of kenosis.

It is plain that, when we confess God as Omnipotent only, we have gained but a half-knowledge of Him; His is an Omnipotence which can at the same time swathe Itself in infirmity and can become the captive of Its own creatures. He has, if I may so speak, the incomprehensible power of even making Himself weak.[64]

In the tradition of kenosis thought reaching back to Saint Paul, Newman makes this reflection on the mystery of God's acceptance of limitation the basis of an appeal for humility among believers. The self-emptying of Christ is the very antithesis of that sin of pride that is the root of this world's fall. The Christ had undone by his acceptance of bondage what Satan had brought about because of his striving after equality with God.

If, then, the very principle of sin is insubordination, is there not a stupendous meaning in the fact, that He, the Eternal, who alone is sovereign and supreme, has given us an example in His own Person of that love of subjection which in Him alone is simply voluntary, but in all creatures is an elementary duty? [65]

There had been recaptured in the piety and preaching of the Roman Catholic Church the richness of the kenotic motif, even though it had largely been lost to its formal theology. There is the emphasis upon the humanity and sufferings of Christ, the voluntary limitation of the divine power, and the practical appeal for a response of humility from the believers. These elements are found in Roman Catholic thought. The kenotic note was never used as it was in Protestantism to help solve the intellectual problems posed by the modern religious consciousness. The Roman Catholic Church was seeking other ways to meet that challenge.

The kenotic motif has played a vital role in the piety and theology of Eastern Orthodoxy. The motif is so widespread as to leave one with an embarrassment of riches. It is a theme found in Russian literature, in the Orthodox liturgy, and in formal theological thought. The theme is so widespread that Nadejda Gorodetzky in a study of nineteenth-century Russian thought refers to a "kenotic mind, or mood, or character," which he says is a cultural ideal shared by the whole nation. The high value placed upon humility, voluntary poverty, self-abasement, and the acceptance of suffering and death in the novels of Gogol, Turgenev, and Dostoevsky are expressions of this "kenotic mood." Although these are not formal theological works, they draw their inspiration for this theme from the picture of Christ in the Gospels and in the Philippian hymn. According to Gorodetzky, this concern for the "kenotic mood" can only be understood through its relation to the unique piety of the Orthodox Church. This does not mean that all the writers who express this mood were formally religious, nor did they all point explicitly to Christ. It is, rather, that they shared in a common cultural tradition whose roots are in a form of

Christian piety stressing the self-emptying and humiliation of Christ. And there is certainly abundant evidence of the centrality of the kenotic motif in the liturgy and preaching of Orthodoxy. This remarkable coincidence between the kenotic motif in the secular and religious literature of Russia illustrates the universality of the motif. It is a motif whose influence extends far beyond any specific theological formula into an ideal for life. It is a motif expressed in liturgy, novel, and poem. The roots of the formal theological thought about kenotic doctrine are in this cultural tradition. The kenotic Christologies developed in Russian thought from the end of the nineteenth century onward spring, not as those of the West from intellectual concerns, but from an ideal deep in culture. The kenotic Christologies of Orthodoxy illustrate the comment of Nicholas Berdyaev that Russian religious philosophy works out subjects raised by Russian literature.

The liturgy and preaching of the Orthodox Church give a large place to the kenotic motif. Typical is the liturgy of Saint Basil in which the priest prays before the consecration:

Thou didst speak unto us by Thy Son Himself . . . who being the brightness of Thy glory and the express image of Thy Person, . . . thought it not robbery to be equal to Thee, the God and Father, but albeit He was God before all ages, yet He was incarnate of the Holy Virgin and did lay aside His godhead, taking the form of a servant, and becoming conformed to the fashion of our lowliness, that He might make us conformable to the image of His glory.[66]

The theme of this prayer is repeated throughout the liturgy, and it came to influence the preaching and teaching of the Orthodox Church greatly. Saint Tykhon (1724–1783) used the moral appeal of Christ's self-emptying as an admonition to charity and asceticism. In his mystical and ascetic writing *True Christianity*, Tykhon urges men to follow the self-emptying of Christ through acts of personal self-denial. It is only through union with Christ in his humility and suffering that men can join in likeness to him in glory. This ideal was also repeated in the preaching of Filaret the Metropolitan, of Moscow (1782–

1867), and other great Orthodox teachers. But it is important to note that these writers and liturgists did not formulate a kenotic doctrine of Christ as such. They were concerned, rather, with the devotional and moral application of the motif.

During the late nineteenth and early twentieth centuries theologians of the Orthodox tradition turned their attention to building formal kenotic Christologies. Although the roots of these Christologies are deep in Russian tradition, the stimulus for them came from the contact of these theologians with the thought of the Western church. The work of Prof. M. M. Tareev (1866–1934) is quite specifically dependent upon the work of A. B. Bruce. And the Christologies of V. Soloviev (1853–1900) and S. N. Bulgakov (1871–1948) reflect the stimulus of Western thought both philosophical and theological. Soloviev interprets kenosis in light of his conception of world-process in a manner reminiscent of Hegel. Soloviev speaks of the relation of the divine realm and the natural world in terms of a process of divinization of the whole cosmos. The key to understanding this process is Christ. The Christ is the source and norm of the progressive divinization of the cosmos because he first emptied himself so as to become a part of that cosmos. By an act of self-denial the Christ entered the chaos of the natural world to bring order and meaning to it. It is through similar acts of self-denial that the progressive divinization of the universe is accomplished.

S. N. Bulgakov was a vigorous proponent of kenotic Christology. He held that just as the kenotic motif had brought new life to the theology of Protestantism, so it could renew Orthodox theology also. He was, of course, critical of those kenotic theories in Protestantism which tended to jeopardize the full divinity of Christ. The purpose of the kenotic theory, for him, was not doctrinal innovation. It was, rather, an explanation and expansion of the Chalcedonian definition. To accomplish his purpose he makes a far wider application of the kenosis motif than had many of the writers on kenotic theory in Protestantism. Kenosis has importance for the inner life of the

Trinity, creation, and incarnation. Kenosis, for Bulgakov, is not a particular happening that makes incarnation possible. It is a quality of the divine life. Kenosis is rooted in the inner life of the Trinity and becomes evident in the creation and redemption of the world.

Bulgakov pictures the inner life of the Trinity as a vital, living process of mutual self-giving or self-emptying between the Three Persons. This mutual interchange is the source of the divine love. The mutual interchange has its roots in the Father who is the image of love itself. But since his love is not static or self-centered, it gives rise through a process of self-giving to the other members of the Trinity. This begetting of the Son and the Spirit is not a temporal but an eternal act. And such a begetting can be spoken of as a kenosis.

The Sonship is already an eternal kenosis . . . because the Word seems to become wordless (in Himself) and makes Himself the Word of the Father. He becomes poor and sacrificially silent in the bosom of His Father. . . . If, on the side of the Father, there is self-negation in begetting of the Son, the Son is thoroughly emptying Himself when He accepts the passive state of the One who is begotten.[67]

A similar line of thought can be pursued in describing the begetting of the Spirit, which according to Orthodox thought does not involve the Son. In this way the whole inner life of the Trinity can be described by a process of mutual self-limiting or self-giving love. This inner quality of the Trinity is then revealed in the creative and redemptive acts of God.

The Trinity, because of the fullness of its own love, does not need any other creature. As the three Persons love one another, they are complete. But it is the very nature of love to extend itself. The divine love seeks to be realized not only within itself but in another. For this reason divine love becomes the basis of creation. Creation does not mean a lessening of the divine life. But in it God enters a new limiting relationship. God has created something other than himself. The creation of the world means there is another to whom God must be related. With the creation of man this limitation goes even farther — God allows to someone else the freedom that he alone had. The freedom of man is real and leaves, as Bulgakov puts it, " room for a certain risk of unsuccess." The Father now consents to wait until his creation responds freely to him in love. The Son and the Spirit also share this limiting relationship with the world. The Son becomes the means of revealing the Father to men by living a human life. The Son shares the incompleteness of man. The Spirit enters into the creative processes of the world as their source. In this regard the Spirit can be said to share in the becoming of the world and its incompleteness. Thus the Trinity as a whole participates in the creating and redeeming of the world by an act of self-emptying.

The kenosis is supremely revealed in the incarnation. The incarnation is the revelation of the preexistent image of the perfect man Jesus. As such, incarnation has a dual meaning. It is the appearing of the Redeemer. It is also the appearing of the highest achievement of world-process. Incarnation is a kenotic process by which the Eternal Logos empties himself into the humble man, Jesus.

The divine nature of the Logos as the source of life remains unchanged and undiminished in Christ. The humiliation affects not the nature (ousia) but the divine form or image (morphē) which is laid aside by Christ at His Incarnation.[68]

At this point Bulgakov's treatment is similar to that of Luther with its distinction between the divine nature, which is retained, and the divine mode of life, which is laid aside. The life of Jesus is marked by all the infirmities and the ignorance common to all men. In stressing this point, Bulgakov goes beyond Luther in describing the alienation of the incarnate Christ from the divine realm. For not only does Christ suffer weakness and ignorance, he also comes under the power of sin. In bearing the sins of the world, Christ undergoes all the infirmities of a sinner. Christ has become incarnate, not in some perfected humanity, but in sinful flesh. This involvement in sinful flesh is the cause of the limitations under which he suffers. The ignorance and weakness of One who by rights is equal to the Father can only be explained through his free acceptance of sinful flesh.

The omniscience of the Logos takes in Jesus the humble form of obedience. How is it to be reconciled with the personality of the One who claimed His equality with the Father? Only the sin of the world taken by the Incarnate seems to explain such a possibility.[69]

In order to take upon himself the sins of the world, the divine in Christ is so extinguished as to leave only his humanity as the center of his conscious experience.

The kenosis of Christ reaches its high point in his death on the cross. It is not only the humanity of Christ that is here involved but even in a measure his divinity. The divine nature reaches its last and greatest limitation — death. But even this death does not mark the end of kenosis. For his resurrection still is marked by limitation. The glorification of Christ is not self-glorification. Although divine by nature, he does not take this power himself. Instead, he is glorified by God the Father. (Phil. 2:11.) This Bulgakov describes as " kenotic glorification " or " glory in humiliation." This kenosis is even found in the heavenly ministry of the ascended Christ. Although he is now the glorious King, the Christ is still humbling himself and waits for the decision of man's freedom. All nature is still groaning in travail until it is released from the final enemy, which is death. Kenosis will not end until the Last Day when death is overcome and all things are restored to their harmony with the divine Wisdom.

The kenotic Christologies of the Orthodox theologians have been little known in Protestant circles. Save for the attention of some Anglican theologians, these Christologies have had no real influence on Protestant theology. Certain other aspects of the thought of Soloviev and Bulgakov have received limited attention, but the constructive possibilities in their kenotic doctrine have largely been unnoticed. Certain features of the thought of the Orthodox, especially Bulgakov, point in a creative direction. First, Bulgakov recognizes that the kenotic motif is important for the whole doctrine of God and creation. Its importance cannot be properly understood if interpreted only in relation to incarnation. Such a limited and one-sided interpretation of kenosis inevitably runs into the impasse that affected Protestant kenotic doctrine. Bulgakov by his broad spectrum of concern points in a direction that any future kenosis doctrine must take. The only way in which kenosis can become intelligible is as a quality of the whole divine life and economy. Second, the Orthodox theologians see self-limitation as a normal part of the divine life, not as a defect that threatens the divine life. This gives the Orthodox a far greater freedom than the mediating theologians of Protestantism in picturing the depth and completeness of Christ's self-emptying. The mediating theologians were always faced by the problem of showing how Christ was still in some sense divine although limited. For the Orthodox, this posed less of a problem because limitation was in a real way part of the life of God. Thus Bulgakov can picture kenosis as embracing even the preearthly and the post-earthly life of Christ. While holding to the language of the Chalcedonian formula, Bulgakov was able to move with far greater freedom than his Protestant contemporaries in its reconstruction.

CHAPTER VIII

The Paradox of Kenosis

THE KENOTIC MOTIF IN CONTEMPORARY THEOLOGY

The Servant Form and the Paradox of Revelation

In the conclusion of the treatment of English kenotic Christologies with Temple's solemn warning of unavoidable and insolvable problems, it would have seemed that the end of the study had been reached. But such a conclusion, although made by many theologians, is premature. It overlooks the manifold, creative possibilities in the kenotic motif. The impasse of these Christologies in the mediating theologians pointed to the end of one dominant tradition of kenotic thought. But fresh approaches to the kenosis question were soon to be opened in the thought of Søren Kierkegaard (1813–1855). Although Kierkegaard was a man of the nineteenth century, he was a prophet so little heard in his own day while so heralded in our day that it seemed best to consider his Christology as a prelude to contemporary thought. For like one "born out of due time," Kierkegaard had no influence on the Christological thinking of his day. It has only been in the twentieth century that his witness has been heard. For although he was a trenchant critic of both the mediating and Hegelian traditions in theology, his witness to the paradoxical and irrational in the faith was overlooked. Instead, theologians bent their efforts on rationalizing or, where this failed, on forgetting the paradoxical elements in Christianity. It was only as the great theological systems of the nineteenth century started to topple that Kierkegaard's voice could be heard. At the core of his message is a bold assertion of the self-emptying of the Christ who meets men as a man. God in the servant form is at the center of Kierkegaard's thought. From this viewpoint the kenotic motif reentered theological thought in the twentieth century.

The setting of the kenotic motif in Kierkegaard is not the doctrine of the Trinity, nor the two natures, nor even the problem of Jesus' consciousness. It is, rather, found initially in the *Philosophical Fragments* in his consideration of how men can know the truth. The focus is upon the consciousness of the believer in his relation to truth rather than on some historical or speculative reconstruction of Jesus' self-consciousness. Hence, the kenosis is cast in a completely different light. It is for him not a principle of intelligibility by which to solve historical or philosophical problems posed for Christianity by modern thought. This was the function of the kenotic motif to the mediating and Hegelian theologians. Rather, kenosis is the absolute paradox over which all attempts to rationalize Christianity stumble and fall. The kenotic motif is found in the thought of Kierkegaard not because it fulfills a need in some system of thought. It is there because he believes it to be first and foremost a basic aspect of the revelation of God in Christ. Kenosis expresses the paradox of Christianity, namely, God has assumed the form of a servant. God has become a man. God on his own initiative has overcome the "infinitely qualitative contradiction" between himself and man.[70] This is the central fact to which all faith must hold.

The background of Kierkegaard's understanding of kenosis is his analysis of the problem of knowledge and divine revelation. He approaches this in the *Philosophical Fragments* through what he calls an experiment in thought. He follows out in thought several possible ways in which men can know the truth. The first major possibility is the Socratic one. In it man is pictured as already having the truth within himself. The function of the teacher is to aid him in the recollection of this truth. In this Socratic scheme man is never really in error. He is simply in a state of forgetfulness. Over against the Socratic scheme Kierkegaard envisages another possibility, namely, that man is really in error. Man does not merely forget the truth. He does not possess the truth, nor even have any intimation of it. Further, he suggests, man is not simply in a state of error; his error is one for which he is responsible. Error means he is really in a state of sin. Therefore, what man needs to attain the truth is not a stimulus to recollection but transformation by a Savior.

This second possibility describes the situation of man as understood by Christian faith. The problem is how can man as sinner come into a relation with God, the Truth? It is to this problem that Kierkegaard directs his analysis. In the light of the "infinitely qualitative contradiction" between God and man, how can man reach knowledge of the truth? The answer is that a way must be found to overcome the chasm between God and man. Man cannot do this himself. Man does not have the capacity for receiving the truth. Even this must be given him. So the only possibility is that God will overcome the gulf between himself and man. God will become the Teacher who creates the conditions for learning the truth. But making this assertion does not prove that God will act to close this gap through a self-limitation. There are still other possibilities for closing the gap with which Kierkegaard experiments.

There is the possibility of the elevation of man, the learner, to the same level as God, the Teacher. Man could be transfigured into something quite unlike himself. And in this transformed state, on the same level as God, he could know God. However, if this were to happen, man would no longer be man. So this possibility is rejected.

There is also the possibility of God's appearing in all his glory and overwhelming man by a divine apparition. Man would forget himself and be swallowed up in the vision of God. But again, man would no longer be man. So the initial terms of the proposition would be unfulfilled. It is man as man who is the learner, not man changed into something other than himself. Having foreclosed these possibilities in his experiment in thought, Kierkegaard comes to the only remaining one: namely, God descends to man. God in a free act of self-emptying becomes a man. Through this act God can come into union with man without destroying man. Man remains man, even as he comes to a knowledge of God. Such is the final measure of God's love for man. It is that man is received into fellowship with God as man. To accomplish this, God assumes the servant form in Jesus Christ.

Since we found that the union could not be brought about by an elevation, it must be attempted by a descent. Let the learner be x. In this x we must include the lowliest. . . . In order that the union may be brought about, God must therefore become the equal of such a one, and so he will appear in the likeness of the humblest. But the humblest is one who must serve others, and God will therefore appear in the form of a servant.[71]

The servant form is not a superficial disguise which God uses to fool man. It is the "profoundest incognito almightily maintained." [72]

For this is the unfathomable nature of love, that it desires equality with the beloved, not in jest merely, but in earnest and truth. And it is the omnipotence of the love which is resolved that it is able to accomplish its purpose.[73]

Because God has accepted this form freely and fully, his life is now one of suffering. The Servant suffers hunger, thirst, agony, and death. The divine love that gives all for others is itself in want.

Kierkegaard rejects all attempts to blunt the scandal of the servant form. It is not that God has become somehow *Man* in a generic or abstract sense. God has become an individual man. The servant form does not mean that God has become a great or heroic man; God has become a suffering and dying man. The self-emptying is complete.

In his approach to kenosis in its relation to the question of divine revelation, Kierkegaard was involved in polemics. In showing the impossibility of man's being elevated to the level of God, he was speaking against Hegelianism and mysticism. He rejects the possibility of man's evolving as part of world-process into the divine life (Hegelianism). He also rejects the possibility of the mystical vision in which the individuality of man is swallowed up in the infinity of God (mysticism). Both these approaches imperil the reality of man as man. To Kierkegaard the final measure of God's love is that God loves man for what he is. Kenosis is the link relating the finitude and sinfulness of man to the love of God. It is important to remember that the kenotic motif does not increase the rational coherence of the Christian faith. Really, its effect is just the opposite. The acceptance by God of the servant form is the final measure of the offense of Christianity. For in becoming a man, the Eternal God has become a particular historical fact. God has done what by every rational conception of his nature he cannot do. He became unlike himself. He became a man and yet remains God. This is an assertion which cannot be rationalized into a doctrine of God-manhood in the style of the Hegelians. It contains as its core a contradiction that cannot be overcome.

Kierkegaard's position on kenosis had wrought a revolution. For as the kenotic motif entered the contemporary theological scene through his writings, its whole function and meaning were changed. It is no longer a principle of intelligibility. It is the paradox of grace. Its importance derives from its central place in revelation rather than its value in solving intellectual problems. There is in Kierkegaard no pondering about the loss or change of divine attributes. He does not speculate about the divine-human consciousness of Christ. Instead, he makes of kenosis the bold paradoxical assertion of God's sovereignty, which brings all speculation to an end. He had taken the kenotic motif from the hands of his opponents to use it against them. His legacy to future students of the motif was a mixed one. While elevating the kenosis to a place of central importance, he cut off the possibility of further describing it.

Kenosis in the Theology of Brunner and Barth

In the theological revolution starting with the early work of Karl Barth after the First World War a new climate of opinion was created in which the kenotic motif could be reconsidered. Two features of this new climate are particularly important for the new kenotic doctrines that were to arise. First, these new theologians, following the lead of Kierkegaard, accepted paradox as an inescapable part of theological thinking. This means speculative difficulties connected with the kenotic motif do not exclude it from theological consideration. The whole speculative attempt is called into question, rather than the kenotic motif as such. The new theology did not look to the motif as a principle of intelligibility for its systems of thought. The kenotic motif was accepted as part of the given of revelation. Second, there is renewed interest in making theology truly Biblical. If a theology is to be Biblical, it must give attention to the kenotic motif. The motif is central to the Biblical message.

It was against this background that Emil Brunner's first book on Christology, *The Mediator*, appeared in 1927. Brunner's approach to kenosis here is marked by polemic concerns and remains largely negative in character. He was often arguing against the older kenotic Christologies he saw remaining on the theological horizon. He criticizes kenotic doctrine on the grounds that it is an illicit attempt to rationalize the mystery of Christ's person. His rejection of the kenotic Christologies in the mediating and Hegelian traditions is part of his larger rejection of all philosophical attempts to rationalize Christian doctrine. The true approach to the person of Christ is one of decision and obedience rather than explanation and theory. Philosophizing about the person of Christ can become a way of avoiding Christ's call to decision and faith. Brunner brings under particular attack the attempts of the kenotic Christologies of the nineteenth century to provide a rational psychology of the God-man. He argues with cogency that the very question of a psychological interpretation of the divine-human consciousness is a contradiction in terms. The only consciousness of which we have any knowledge is a human consciousness. The only patterns for interpreting consciousness derive from a knowledge of the human mind, a knowledge that in itself is limited. When the question of a divine-human consciousness is broached, we move into an area in which we have no knowledge. Analogies from human consciousness may be as misleading as helpful.

At this early stage Brunner gives scant attention to the constructive possibilities in the kenotic motif. He does not use the motif as a way of explaining the incarnation. There is no discussion of how kenosis makes the incarnation possible. Rather, the motif is used to interpret Jesus' earthly ministry. Kenosis concerns the degree of divine self-manifestation or self-veiling in Christ during his earthly ministry. Specifically, Brunner treats the question raised by New Testament scholarship whether Jesus actually made Messianic claims for himself. He holds that Jesus did not make the high claims for himself made later by the church because he was " in the form of a servant." During the earthly ministry there was a " divine incognito " that veiled partially the fully divine nature of Christ. This " incognito " was an evidence of the divine self-limitation which characterized the life of Jesus. The high claims made for his divinity later by the church could be made only in light of the cross and resurrection. Yet the divine self-emptying or incognito was not so complete that Jesus made no Messianic claims for himself. He made claims to a unique office. But the claims were veiled in language that could be understood only from the standpoint of faith.

In the second volume of his *Dogmatics*, 1949, Brunner gives further and more constructive attention to the kenotic motif. This time he approaches the kenosis in relation to the incarnation itself, instead of only to the earthly ministry of Jesus. Yet even now his treatment is marked by a reserve in speculating about the divine life. He warns that the kenotic passages in the New Testament do not tell how the incarnation took place. They simply witness to the fact of the incarnation. According to the New Testament, kenosis does mean that Christ laid aside the divine attributes of omnipotence and omniscience in becoming incarnate. Incarnation is a self-limitation of God. The

exact extent of this self-limitation remains unknown. There are
only very general limits that can be set to it. On one side,
kenosis means a divine self-limitation that still makes it possible
to speak of Jesus as divine. On the other side, kenosis means a
divine self-limitation that makes it possible to speak of Jesus as
a true man. Jesus can rightfully be said to have "a human
historical personality." With these assertions Brunner is willing
to let the question rest.

In the *Dogmatics* he also carries forward the earlier emphasis
on kenosis as a characteristic of Jesus' earthly life. Jesus' life of
humble obedience, which reached its high point on the cross,
is an evidence of the divine self-limitation. But this kenosis
shown by Jesus' acts of humility and obedience is not an obscuring of the divine presence. It is, rather, the revelation of
God under the conditions of human life.

It is not in spite of the Cross, in spite of its evident "weakness," in
spite of human impotence and frailty, that He reveals Himself to us
as the Son of God, but particularly on the Cross. It is precisely the
folly of the Cross which is the wisdom of God, it is precisely the
exinanitio, the extreme point of the *kenosis*, which is the supreme
height of the self-manifestation of God.[74]

Kenosis is the supreme paradox of Christian faith. For in the
moment of weakness, when the divine power seems completely
obscured, it is supremely revealed. God is Lord in all things,
even the suffering and death of the man on the cross who is his
Son.

There are two points at which Brunner's treatment of Christology makes an important contribution to rethinking the kenotic motif. First, he sees the self-emptying of God in Christ as
a means of revealing and not merely of obscuring the divine.
The older kenotic Christologies had been so concerned with
showing how a divine limitation made possible a human personality, they had forgotten the possibility of divine revelation
under the conditions of human life. Second, the method of
approaching the meaning of kenosis is changed. Negatively,
Brunner has rejected the notion that kenosis is the basis of a

rational explanation of the incarnation. We do not possess adequate intellectual *schēma* to discern the exact nature of the divine self-emptying. Yet this does not mean the kenosis question cannot be investigated. Thinking about kenosis must proceed from the reality of the divine revelation in Christ rather than as a means of establishing the possibility of such a revelation. To use the logical term, thinking about kenosis must be a posteriori not a priori. The starting point for thought about kenosis is the witness of Scripture that such an act has occurred, not an ontological or psychological explanation of the possibility of such an act. Given the appearance of God in Jesus Christ as witnessed to in Scripture, it is possible to ask significant questions about kenosis. The answers to the questions about kenosis can never be final or definitive. But the question can be fruitfully pursued from this new perspective. However, up to this time, Brunner has not chosen to elaborate more fully on the start he made in this new direction.

Karl Barth approaches the kenotic motif in a bold and discerning manner. His analysis of it in a commentary on Philippians and in his *Dogmatics* is the most extensive on the contemporary scene. The motif has a creative role in his doctrine of God, of Christ, and of reconciliation. In Barth's theology, kenosis assumes its place as a major motif of Christian faith. It appears and reappears to shape Christian doctrine in a variety of ways. There is a comprehensiveness and subtilty of thought on this question which belies any brief treatment. For Barth has grasped more clearly than any of his contemporaries the basic and all-pervasive importance of kenosis in Christian revelation.

Any interpretation of Barth's doctrine must come to terms with one basic fact. His approach to the kenotic motic, as indeed his approach to any theological question, is shaped decisively by his own particular brand of theologizing. As problematic as this method appears in the eyes of many, it remains the inescapable starting point of Barth's thought. So for the moment, without arguing the merits or defects of his methodology in the abstract, its functional importance for his thought must be recognized and accepted. It can be judged later by its fruits. To put the matter briefly, Barth's approach is systematic, starting with the revelation of God in Christ as witnessed to by Scripture. He does not approach the kenotic motif as a principle of intelligibility with which to solve doctrinal problems. Nor does he analyze it from the standpoint of some generally accepted notion of the divine being, nor some supposedly historical reconstruction of Jesus' self-consciousness. The question of kenosis becomes a matter of concern for him because it is part of the given of revelation. There has been a divine self-emptying in Christ. Scripture witnesses to this self-emptying. On the basis of this witness the nature and meaning of kenosis can be investigated. All thinking about kenosis proceeds from the assumption that the kenosis is a reality. The task of theology is to interpret its meaning in a full and systematic way.

The basic lines of Barth's approach to the motif are seen in his commentary, *Erklärung des Philipperbriefes*, 1933. Here he sets about trying to right an all to prevalent misunderstanding of kenosis. Kenosis, says Barth, is not a matter of a loss in divinity. To approach it in such a manner is to be misled. The reality of God in Christ is not in some way scaled down to a level compatible with human life. To say this would be to make the incarnation the downgrading of God. Kenosis is the affirmation that God is Lord even in his humiliation. God is God as equally in the hiddenness of the servant form as in the fullness of his transcendent glory. The whole message of the Philippian hymn is that in becoming man God did not become unlike himself. If God is God only in transcendent glory, he is not really Lord of all. The God who is Lord of all is Lord, even in the form of a suffering, dying man. The divine self-emptying is the highest affirmation of the Lordship of God. It is the affirmation that the realm of sinful humanity is not foreign to God. It is under his Lordship. The exaltation of Christ of which Philippians speaks is the tearing away of the veil obscuring Christ's true glory. The exaltation reveals to all men what has always been true, even in its hiddenness: Jesus Christ is Lord!

The extensive development of the kenotic motif throughout the *Dogmatics* is essentially derived from the insight given in this early commentary. The task of a theology of kenosis may be stated very simply. It is to interpret the meaning of the statement: God is Lord, even in the servant form. What does it imply about the nature of God? What does it say about the nature of man? How does this shape our understanding of the person and work of Christ? These are the manifold questions with which the student of kenosis must be concerned. To ask the questions of kenosis is not to deal with a single isolated aspect of Christian revelation. It is to deal with a basic feature of this revelation.

In his search for the full meaning of kenosis, Barth shows himself to be a keen student of the history of Christian thought. He has looked at the many attempts of kenosis doctrines in the past. He has patiently analyzed their errors and failings. He has realistically found the important values and insights these past efforts enshrined. He studied the mediating theologians of the nineteenth century, particularly Thomasius and Dorner, with an active sympathy he does not always accord to thinkers of that era. And from his study he believes the verdict of history is clear. If the kenotic motif is to be understood, the existing patterns of thought about God cannot be used. They are simply unable to express the kenosis properly. What is implied by the kenotic motif is a major reconstruction of the doctrine of God.

To follow Barth in his reconstruction, it is first necessary to know what he has rejected in past doctrines of God. To state this critique in blanket form, it is the rejection of " natural theology." By " natural theology " he means all attempts to establish through reason and experience a generally accepted notion of what God " is." For him, the only source of a knowledge of God is revelation. The contrast between these sources of knowledge is absolute. Barth reads the history of theology in terms of a struggle between the knowledge of God given in revelation and the supposed knowledge of him found in human wisdom and experience. When some philosophical idea of God predominates in a theology, the unique notion of God found in revelation is muted or perverted. Such a theology can be said to be dominated by a "natural theology." The task of a sound theology is to overcome this dominance. Divine revelation is to be understood in terms of itself.

The difficulties brought into the doctrine of God by "natural theology" are no more clearly revealed than in relation to the kenosis. The basic error of the patristic doctrine of God derived from its use of a "natural theology," namely, its reliance on the Greek notion of being. The living God of Scripture cannot be comprehended in terms of changeless being. A divine self-emptying becomes nonsense within such a doctrine of God. This difficulty had been discerned already by the mediating theologians of the last century. And Barth joins them eloquently in their critique. But he pushes farther to see what were the failures of the mediating theologians in their attempted reconstructions. Again he sees the problem as basically one of "natural theology." This time the difficulty stems from a doctrine of God too dependent upon the theory of being of idealism. The mediating theologians made the mistake of proceeding in their theologizing in an a priori manner. Instead of starting from the reality of revelation, they started from what they thought to be generally valid notions about God. From this basis they wanted to explain the possibility of revelation through some form of divine self-emptying. The final result, though, was always the same — an impasse that denied either the humanity of Christ or the absoluteness of God.

Barth does not pause with this general analysis of the shortcomings of the mediating theologians. Believing, as he does, that these theologians came near to the heart of the matter in their kenosis doctrines, he looks more closely into their teachings. The point he uncovers is an important one in his own doctrine of God. Specifically, he says, the mediating theologians were misled by making a false division between the divine being and the divine action. They made the mistake of separating their understanding of God's inner life from God's action. Nowhere is this tendency more clear than in their teatment of kenosis. They tried to describe the changes in the inner life of the Trinity that would make kenosis possible. But no matter how adroit were these theories, they always came to grief. They made the divine action somehow seem strange or extraneous to the divine being. It was as if God had to readjust himself laboriously to the task of self-limitation. Was it not somehow closer to the truth, Barth asks, to say being and action are one in God? The free acceptance of limitation is of the very nature of God. It is not an extraneous happening to which God must adjust.

The prime feature of Barth's doctrine of God is the assertion of the unity of being and act. God is who he is in the act of revelation.[75] God does not stand apart from his actions. The revealing act of God in Christ is not something foreign to his inner life as God. Revelation is not an action to which the divine being had to adjust. It is of the very being of God to reveal himself. Scripture never speaks of God as the silent, mysterious Something that stands apart from the world of action and life. God is who he is because he acts in this world of men and events. So in his description of the being of God, the word "event" or "act" is final and inescapable. God's being is a being in act. God is not ultimately something different from his revelation.

From such a starting point the first major assertion about the being of God becomes evident. God is the living God. His being is life. Since God reveals himself in the event of Christ, i.e., in a life, he is himself life. God cannot be understood in terms of the changeless or lifeless. God is not to be spoken of as if he were somehow beyond the change and variability of living. Conceiving God as changeless being is an error that has troubled Christian thought from the patristic period onward. Such a description is already a giant step toward atheism. To say God is beyond all change is finally to say God is dead. Scripture speaks of the living God who meets men in decisive acts. This bespeaks a creative variety in the life of God. There

is in the being of God all the change, vitality, and responsive-
ness of life.

To make this assertion of the living God is neither unique
nor without its problems, as Barth clearly sees. Many theologians of the mediating and the Hegelian traditions made
just such assertions. Yet these theologies failed because of their
inability to conceive properly the divine independence and absoluteness. The Hegelians, for example, gave eloquent testimony
to vitality and change in the divine life. But they explained
this change by making God dependent upon the world. In their
schemes God needed the world to complete his own being.
This, Barth rejects in the name of Biblical revelation. He wishes
to find instead a way of combining the ideas of change and
vitality in the divine being with those of constancy and absoluteness. How can God be spoken of as the living God in
active, responsive relations to the world and yet as constant?
How can God be intimately related to the world and yet ultimately independent of it? These questions have never been
answered adequately in any of the available doctrines of God.
Yet answers to them are of basic importance if sense is to be
made of kenosis. For these are the issues involved in any kenosis
doctrine.

Barth deals constructively with these questions in his treatment of the divine perfection in the *Dogmatics* II, 1. In this
section he deals with what has traditionally been called the
attributes of God. Since the term " attributes " is itself misleading in many respects, they are spoken of here as the perfections of God. These perfections fall into two groups: the perfections of the divine loving and the perfections of the divine
freedom. Knowledge of these perfections is gained through reflection upon the revelation of God in his Word. Such reflections reveal two basic features of the divine being. The being
of God is love. The being of God is being in freedom. These
two assertions become the key to understanding how God com-
bines in himself both constancy and change, both relatedness
and independence. The answers to these questions lie in the

way the divine love and the divine freedom relate to one another.

The being of God can be defined as the being of one who loves. " God is He who in His Son Jesus Christ loves all His children, in His children all men, and in men His whole creation." [76] The expression of this love is the creation of fellowship between God and man. This loving fellowship is the underlying aim of creation and redemption. Man and the world were created by God for fellowship with him. They are redeemed by God to remove the last barrier to full and free fellowship — the barrier of sin. But in all this, God is not dependent on man. God is already complete in himself. He does not need to love us. He is love already within himself. God's love implies, rather, an overflow of his essence, which he turns toward us and creates with us a fellowship of redemptive love. In other words, God's loving is a loving in freedom. God is not bound to love us. He is free to love us. God always remains who he is even while seeking fellowship with men. This is the quality which sets the divine loving apart from all other forms of love. Human love is inevitably dependent. Men need to love to preserve their very beings. Man's being is modified by the ones he loves. Human love lacks freedom. The perfection of the divine love by contrast is its freedom. God is free to have fellowship with man. But in this fellowship God does not become unlike himself. He still remains God the Lord.

The consideration of the divine loving has led to the affirmation of the divine freedom. God's love is a love in freedom. Having reflected on the divine love, Barth moves to a closer definition of the divine freedom. For him it has a twofold meaning.

The divinity of the freedom of God consists and confirms itself in the fact that in Himself and in all His works God is One, constant and eternal, and therewith also omnipresent, omnipotent and glorious. [77]

The divine freedom may be defined negatively as God's freedom from external influences. Because he is free in this sense, God

is constant or eternal. But the divine freedom also has a positive character. It means God is free to enter fully into realities
different from himself. God is free to relate to others and yet
never become unlike himself. The divine freedom means not
simply isolation from the world. It also means freedom for complete involvement in the world. God is free to indwell the world
as its Creator. He is free to share fully in the life of man to
become his Redeemer. Yet in all these relations he does not
become unlike himself. In all he remains God the Lord who
can be spoken of as omnipresent, omnipotent, and glorious.

From this analysis of the divine love and freedom the absoluteness of God can be defined more clearly. The divine absoluteness is obviously not in his changelessness or unrelatedness.
Rather, it is God's freedom to fulfill his will of love for man
and the world. God's absoluteness means two things: First,
there is no external force that can frustrate or destroy God's
will to loving fellowship with his creation. The great constant
— the eternal factor — in the divine life is the unswerving will
of love. It is a will of love that even human sin cannot destroy.
Secondly, in entering close and full relation to man and the
world as Creator and Redeemer, God does not become unlike
himself. His relatedness does not compromise his basic being.
It is actually integral to his being of love to be related to creation. God is who he is in his relations to the world as well as
in his transcendence over the world. As Barth never wearies of
saying: God is, in all things, God the Lord. In transcendent
glory or in the form of a dying man upon a cross, God is Lord.
He is absolute in his full and free relation of love to men.

From this standpoint it is possible to interpret Barth's use
of the kenotic motif. This background was necessary because
his kenosis doctrine takes its unique form from his doctrine of
God. Kenosis is the divine self-emptying or self-limitation by
which God fulfills his will of love for man. Kenosis is the divine
self-limitation by which God comes into redemptive relationship with men as a man. In response to his love for man, God
acts freely to accept existence as a man. But in so doing, God

does not become unlike himself. Kenosis is an expression of the divine loving and the divine freedom. God remains absolute and immutable in his self-emptying in Christ because it is the supreme fulfillment of his will of love for men.

From his study of the older kenotic doctrines, Barth saw their central problem was the inability to picture how God could accept limitation and still remain the absolute, sovereign God. He meets this problem now by defining the divine absoluteness or constancy in terms of God's ability to enter every relationship and yet remain unchanged. First and foremost, God is constant because of his unswerving will of love for men. But because God is free he is not limited to expressing this will in only one particular way. God is not bound to a set plan in his search for fellowship with his creation. Instead, God is capable of infinite individual variation in his relations to the world. At one pont, in a typical moment of theological whimsy, Barth suggests that it is perhaps misleading to speak of God's "immutability." In reality, it is man who is "immutable" in his sin. God has a "holy mutability" in his relations with man and the world. In the drama of human salvation God alone is fully free in the fulfillment of his eternal will of love. Kenosis is one of the ways God fulfills this purpose. It is one of the divine stratagems by which God brings men into fellowship with himself.

Kenosis is the supreme measure of God's freedom for man. In his revelation in Christ, God is free for us men. He is free to be our God without ceasing to be God the Lord. Nowhere does the sovereign freedom of God shine forth more clearly than in the moment God becomes, as it were, "God for us a second time" in his becoming the man Christ Jesus.

The miracle of the Incarnation . . . is seen when we realize that the Word of God descended from the freedom, majesty, and glory of His divinity, that without becoming unlike Himself He assumed likeness to us, and that now He is to be sought and found of us here, in his human being.[78]

God as men encounter him in Christ is not God scaled down to meet the measure of man. God in Christ is God the transcendent One who is also the humiliated One. The core of self-identity that links the transcendent and the humbled God is his loving freedom to redeem man. A self-emptying of God is possible that does not vitiate his absoluteness precisely because self-emptying fulfills his redemptive purpose. Kenosis is not the loss of full divinity by the Son. It is, rather, the clearest revealing of that divinity.

The way of the Son of God into the far country, i.e., into the lowliness of creaturely being, of being as man, into unity and solidarity with sinful and therefore perishing humanity, the way of His Incarnation is as such the activation, the demonstration, the revelation of His deity, His divine Sonship.[79]

Barth's interpretation of the kenotic motif is marked by two basic changes from that of the mediating theologians which have proved fruitful. First, Barth has changed the method of approach to the question of the kenosis. He rejects the attempts to think in an a priori manner. In the past, kenosis has been approached along these lines: knowing what we do about God, how can we conceive a divine self-emptying? Barth's approach is a posteriori. He proceeds by asking: in the light of the self-emptying of God in Christ, what can be said about the nature of God and man? Second, Barth interprets kenosis as an integral part of the divine being. Kenosis is not a special event in the divine life. It is a basic characteristic of the divine being. By treating kenosis as an expression of the absoluteness of God, he avoids the impasse of the kenotic Christologies of the past. According to Barth, God is who he is because of his kenosis. For many of the mediating theologians, God is who he is in spite of his kenosis.

Barth treats the kenotic motif in two other connections. In the *Dogmatics* I, 2, he relates the kenosis to the doctrine of the impersonal human nature of Christ. He attempts to rework this doctrine which has fallen on such evil days in modern times. His treatment here is reminiscent of the older orthodoxy. But the interests he is trying to preserve are real. His point is that the human nature which Christ assumed did not constitute a limit to his divinity because his human nature became personal only through a union with the Logos. The divine self-emptying does not mean the Logos is subsumed under the powers of an already existing personality. Although there is a kenosis of the Logos, his life in the flesh is still a life determined fully by God. Kenosis must never be construed to mean a limitation of the divine life. It is a reexpression of the divine being in another form. The humanity of Christ is real, but it is humanity used as a vehicle for divine revelation. As important as this point may be, it is not without its difficulties as stated here. Unfortunately, Barth is not entirely specific on this point. But he seems to come close here to losing the reality of Jesus' humanity, which he so vigorously expounds in other places.

The second place at which the kenotic motif is found is the doctrine of reconciliation. (*Dogmatics* IV, 1 and IV, 2.) The general framework of the doctrine is set within the contrast between the Lord as Servant and the Servant as Lord. Barth uses the kenotic motif here to interpret the work of Christ as in previous sections he used it to interpret Christ's person. The divine self-emptying is a symbol of the whole movement of God toward man. The Lord as Servant reaches out to sinful man to reestablish fellowship with him. The exaltation of the Servant as Lord is a symbol of the answering response of the men who have been redeemed. "The Way of the Son of God into the far country" is the title given to God's reconciling work in the atoning death of Christ. "The homecoming of the Son of Man" is the response of the men who have been made new in Christ. The Cristological motif of self-emptying and exaltation can be legitimately applied here because in reconciliation all its aspects have actuality in Jesus Christ. Christ is both God seeking man and man responding to God. What can be said of the person of Christ — namely, that he is the subject of both self-emptying and exaltation — can also be said of his work. The person and work of Christ are not two different things. They are two aspects of the same thing. They are comprised by the call of God and the response of man.

Any evaluation of Barth's kenosis doctrine, as indeed of any part of his theology, is linked with the answer to a prior question. What is your attitude toward his method of theologizing? In his approach Barth has brought about a major shift in kenosis doctrine. But this shift is directly linked with his method, specifically, his rejection of all "natural theology." Much he says about kenosis stands or falls with his methodology. A closer look has to be taken at it in the next chapter. For the moment certain things are clear even for those who question it. The shift from a priori to a posteriori analysis of the kenotic motif has been productive. It has allowed Barth to ask more fruitful questions than had many previous interpreters of the motif. Through his reconstruction of the doctrine of God he has avoided the fatal division between act and being that contributed so heavily to the failure of the mediating theologies of kenosis. The interpretation of kenosis as an expression of the divine loving and the divine freedom marks a decisive break with the older static ontologies. In his use of love and freedom as the basic categories for the doctrine of God, Barth has rendered the kenosis a good deal more intelligible. Yet major questions remain.

In the doctrine of God how does Barth account for the divine freedom? At times he treats the divine freedom as if it were a basic quality of the divine life. The divine freedom is simply a fact. It is a basic datum for the doctrine of God that cannot be further explained. Yet at other times, Barth explains the divine freedom by the traditional argument from God's own inner-relatedness. God is free to relate to others and yet remain constant because he is first inner-related himself as Father, Son, and Holy Spirit. But such a line of thought leads right back to the difficulties of the past. How can the Son be both limited and still a full member of the Trinity?

The question must also be raised as to how Barth's treatment of kenosis relates to the New Testament. By virtue of
his theological method he is committed to reading the Biblical
witness in terms of itself. Yet his exegesis of Phil. 2:5-11 and
II Cor. 8:9 raises questions at just this point. His treatment of
these kenotic passages shows far greater affinities with the traditional exegesis than to a fully historical analysis. Admittedly,
it is necessary for the theologian to go beyond the historical
scholar in the use of Biblical materials. The concerns of theology extend beyond linguistic analysis and the study of literary
and mythological background. But it is not possible for the
theologian to go beyond the findings of historical scholarship
by overlooking them. Although Barth's exegesis of the kenotic
passages is often insightful, it overlooks some of the most important results of historical scholarship. In his exegesis he interprets these passages in the light of later developments of
Trinitarian doctrine not found in the New Testament itself.
Specifically, he makes the status of the Logos before and after
the earthly life of Jesus the same. The exaltation of Christ is
given no place. Yet the New Testament clearly contains the
element of exaltation to a new and higher status for the Christ
because of his earthly ministry. Historical study has shown it
was only later Trinitarian doctrine that made the preexistent
and exalted Christ of equal status. Barth does not recognize
this anachronism in his thought or try to provide any rationale
for it. Although being an astute historian of doctrine in many
respects, he is unwilling to go behind the Trinitarian formulas
to read the New Testament historically. Rather, he follows the
tradition of orthodoxy from the days of Athanasius and Victorinus to our own. He reads the New Testament as a proof
text for a Trinitarianism that it contains only fragmentarily.

CHAPTER IX

Kenosis in a New Key

A RESTATEMENT OF THE KENOTIC MOTIF

The Legacy of History

The interpretation of the kenotic motif has had a long and involved history. The relation of any modern restatement of the motif to this history will be twofold. Any new formulation must avoid the pitfalls and impasses of the past. But more important it must perceive the creative possibilities that lie dormant in doctrinal history. Such a task is difficult. There is always the temptation to repeat in varying accents what has been said before. There is also the very real danger of impoverishing thought by ignoring what has been said before. Instead, there must be a dialogue with history in order to glimpse afresh the reality of God that stands behind the doctrinal formulas of the past. To ascertain the legacy of history is to take the first step toward reconstruction. This legacy can best be seen if its main features are brought into view through an outline of the history already given in detail.

In the New Testament the kenotic motif is expressed through an idiom shaped by the Jewish-apocalyptic and Hellenistic-Gnostic thought of late antiquity. The motif was unsystematic in form. It was based on the dynamic, personalistic conception of God common to Biblical thought. The motif explains the basic character of God in his act of saving men. Salvation came through the Christ, a preexistent heavenly being, who freely took up human life. His life was one of humble obedience ending in death. He had freely emptied himself of life in the

divine realm for that of a man. For this act of humble obedience he is exalted by God the Father to the new and higher
status of Lord. This Lord is now to be worshiped and served
by all who would be saved. By his self-emptying and subsequent exaltation he had brought salvation to man.

As the church brought its message into relation with the intellectual world of Greco-Roman antiquity, the kenotic motif
was modified in the process of assimilation. The motif was
formulated into a systematic doctrine so as to accord with the
new orthodoxy that emerged in the anti-Arian controversy.
The flexible, unsystematic conception of divine self-emptying
found in the New Testament was reinterpreted through the
static, abstract ontology derived from Greek philosophical
monotheism. The Christ was declared to be fully and un-
changeably divine in his preexistent, earthly, and exalted states.
The New Testament picture of exaltation to a higher status
for the Christ appeared to border on Arianism in the eyes of
the supporters of the new Athanasian orthodoxy. But it soon
became evident in the patristic theology that this assimilation
of the motif into a static conception of God placed it beyond
the pale of intelligibility.

Since God can't change, how is a divine self-emptying to be
explained? The best answer the patristic theologians had was
that the Logos took a human body. Yet this assertion was
hedged about to protect the deity of Christ. His body is human,
as shown by the fact that he ate, drank, slept, and finally died.
Gnosticism had been overcome to this extent at least. Yet the
problem of conceiving a human mental, emotional, and spiritual
life for Jesus remained. As the deity of Christ was conceived
by the fathers, it tended to deny the reality of his human
psychic functions. While avoiding docetism in relation to
Jesus' physical life, they did not avoid a docetic psychology.
In the light of its conception of his deity, orthodoxy could find
no logical place for the ignorance and finitude of a human
mind within Jesus. At best, they could say he had willed to be
ignorant about certain things at certain times.

These problems which beset patristic Christology were not immediately evident. Nor were they to become so for centuries to follow. A docetic psychology did not seem an inconsistency because people inevitably thought of Jesus more in terms of his divinity than of his humanity. It was only with the major shift of religious consciousness in modern times that these questions were to be reopened. The first step toward this reconsideration came with the Reformation in which the importance of Christ's humanity for piety and theology was rediscovered. However, Protestant orthodoxy was never able to explore fully the implications of Christ's humanity. This investigation followed only in the wake of the Enlightenment in the eighteenth century. The new historical interest which arose at that time gave new breadth and depth to the picture of Jesus as a man. The question of Christ's nature had been reopened by these discoveries in a manner more comprehensive than at any time since the fifth century.

With this reopening, the kenotic motif came back into formal theological thought. It was used by theologians of the mediating tradition to act as a bridge between the traditional doctrines of Christ's divinity and the new picture of his humanity. They held that kenosis was an actual limitation accepted by God which made his indwelling of Christ compatible with true humanity. Such assertions of a real divine self-limitation marked the first break with the patristic doctrine of God that had dominated theology to that time. God was not changeless being; he had really limited himself. The problem was to find a way of saying how God could change and yet remain absolute. The mediating theologians redefined the absoluteness of God in terms of his ability to change freely in fulfilling his will of love. This insight marked an important advance in interpreting kenosis, but it was an advance the mediating school was never able to utilize fully. Their thought was stymied through efforts to explain God's self-limitation in terms of rearrangements in the life of the Trinity.

In many respects the Hegelians did an intellectually more

convincing job of stating a kenosis doctrine. They realized
kenosis could not be used to perform a repair job on the sagging structure of orthodoxy. It implied a whole new doctrine
of God. They developed a doctrine of God in which self-
limitation is integral to the divine life. Although able to account for change in the divine life convincingly, the Hegelians
undercut the independence of God.

By the end of the nineteenth century the interpretations of
kenosis by both the mediating and left-wing theologians had
been shown to be inadequate. These interpretations were not
only intellectually unsound but in many respects incompatible
with Biblical thought. No one perceived the roots of this failure
more clearly than P. T. Forsyth. It lay in the inadequate categories of thought used for interpretation. A new personalistic
ontology was needed that conformed more closely to the realities being expressed than had any of the traditional categories of being and nature. Forsyth experimented inconclusively
with such a "metaphysic of faith," but he despaired of giving
kenosis an intellectually satisfactory account. The kenotic motif
was no longer used as a principle of intelligibility to solve
theological problems. Kenosis claimed a place in theology because it was basic to the Biblical picture of Christ.

The kenotic motif entered contemporary theology through
the writings of Kierkegaard, who stressed its paradoxical nature. Kenosis is the absolute paradox that brings to naught all
attempts at giving the faith rational coherence. Since this is
the case, a new method is needed in formulating a doctrine of
kenosis. Thought about it must proceed a posteriori not a priori.
The question to be asked is: Given a divine self-emptying in
Christ, what does this say about the nature of God and man?
Out of this background, contemporary theologians have interpreted kenosis as the expression of God's freedom for man.
Barth has given new systematic statement to kenosis through
his personalistic doctrine of God. God is a free person who in
expressing his will of love for man can accept the limitations
of human life without ceasing to be God.

Three basic factors in the construction of a contemporary statement of kenosis doctrine emerge from history. (1) The methodology for such a constructive restatement is a posteriori. Thinking can most fruitfully proceed from the assumption of a kenosis in Christ to the construction of a doctrine of God and Christology. The starting point must not be some preconceived ontology within which kenosis is to be fitted. Kenosis must be understood in its own terms rather than in those alien to it. (2) Kenosis can only become intelligible in terms of personalistic, dynamic categories of thought. Kenosis is the free act of a personal God and can only be understood in these terms. (3) The kenotic motif cannot be used in the construction of a Christology alone. Kenosis has to form an integral part of the doctrine of God. It is an account of how God acts and what he is like. Hence, kenosis must first be intelligible in the doctrine of God before it can be applied to the person and work of Christ.

The constructive statement of kenosis will involve systematic consideration of these factors. They dictate the structure of the first three sections of the restatement: *The Method of Approach, Ontological Patterns and Biblical Witness,* and *The Doctrine of God.*

The Method of Approach

Two major methodologies have appeared in the construction of kenosis doctrines: a priori and a posteriori. The a priori method has assumed sources of knowledge of ultimate reality from which revelation can be validated and interpreted. Generally this knowledge has taken the form of some rationally verified theory of being. On the basis of the picture of God and man derived from these ontologies, the kenotic motif is investigated. The meaning of a divine self-emptying, even the possibility of such self-emptying, is considered in the light of what is known of the nature of God and man. Prime examples of this method are to be found among the fathers and the theologians of the last century. Sometimes this was done rather explicitly; at others, the assumption remained implicit. These theologians believed their method valid because they held their ontologies to be universally and rationally valid. Hence, they were appropriate for investigating the divine being and action. However, the a priori method of theologizing constantly ran into difficulty when it came to interpreting kenosis. The weakness of the method lies in the limitations of the supposedly universal theories of being from which they proceed. Ontologies are in fact particular and limited in their applicability. The Hellenistic Greek and romantic-idealistic ontologies, for example, have peculiarities that reflect their own assumptions. These ontologies were unable to comprehend many of the features of Biblical thought. Hellenistic thought was unable to interpret the dynamic quality of Biblical thought about God. Idealism was unable to grasp the personal character of God or to interpret his aseity properly. So it was inevitable that the attempts to interpret the Biblical notion of kenosis in such terms would come to naught.

In their polemic against " natural theology " Kierkegaard and Barth have suggested an a posteriori method of theologizing. This modern polemic against " natural theology " has much about it which remains questionable. But it does suggest a new methodological alternative that has proved fruitful, particularly in the case of Barth, for investigating kenosis. The starting point of this method is the assumption of a revelation through Christ that is witnessed to by Scripture. This revelation must be interpreted in its own terms. The task of theology is to begin with revelation and then seek to make it intelligible to the modern world.

The meaning of this a posteriori method can be illustrated in relation to the building of a kenosis doctrine. What is envisaged is primarily a change in the order or priority of questions asked about kenosis. The question of kenosis is no longer: How is kenosis possible in the light of God's nature? The question is rather: What is God's nature in the light of kenosis? Traditionally, the question was asked: How is God-manhood

possible in the light of the nature of God and man? The
a posteriori method suggests the more fruitful question: What
does the reality of Christ's God-manhood tell about the nature
of God and man?

Obviously such a methodological change is never a simple
or complete possibility. In reality the development of any theological statement is the result of a dialogue in which the actuality of revelation is related to philosophical doctrine, church
formulas, and personal experience in a complex manner. There
is no simon-pure theology that proceeds only from revelation
into the task of interpretation. This is true because revelation
does not exist as a specific given body of information in Scripture or anywhere else. Revelation is only known in the event
of its apprehension. And the apprehension of revelation is always conditioned by thought categories that are not in themselves revelation. What the new methodology implies is more
nearly a change in the order of questions asked about theological matters. A posteriori thinking in theology takes its de-
parture from a very commonsense assumption. It believes the
most fruitful basis on which to investigate the meaning of
revelation is from the assumption of its reality. By designating
clearly its subject matter, theology is more able to proceed to
fruitful interpretations.

Such a posteriori thinking is not limited to the use of Biblical
language. Nor does it assume no valid centers of knowledge
about reality outside revelation. This method seeks the co-
ordination of various centers of knowledge. The advent of
process philosophy, for example, with its dynamic ontology can
play a vital part in any contemporary statement of kenosis.
Similarly, modern psychological thought, particularly personality
theory, can be of value in describing a doctrine of the divine
self-emptying. The whole riches of human knowledge can be
bent to the task of apprehending and interpreting revelation.
The difference from the older a priori method is in the priority
of questions to be asked. The basic question for this restatement will be: Assuming the reality of divine kenosis in creation

and redemption, how can this be interpreted through the categories of modern thought?

What is undertaken here can be called in the Kierkegaardian sense "an experiment in thought." Ultimately the fruitfulness of this experiment can only be judged by its result. Can this method of approach bring us closer to an intelligible statement of the divine self-emptying?

Ontological Patterns and Biblical Witness

Basic to any doctrine of kenosis is a picture of God and man. The interpretation of kenosis requires certain minimal presuppositions about the nature of ultimate reality. The problem in all kenosis doctrine has centered in the relation of various ontologies to the Biblical picture of God. Unless an ontology can express the main features of the Biblical picture of God, distortion and intellectual impasse is inevitable. This impasse has developed in relation to the two major ontological patterns found in kenosis doctrine up to the present time — the Greek and the romantic-idealistic. These ontologies have clashed in basic ways with the Biblical motif of the divine self-emptying. Theologians have been aware of these clashes and of the inadequacies of existing patterns of thought about God. They have sought, often with great ingenuity, to modify an ontology so as to bring it into closer conformity with the Biblical witness to God. But in relation to the Greek and the romantic-idealistic ontologies these modifications have not proved satisfactory. The basic features of these ontologies, although permitting the expression of certain aspects of Biblical thought, have also stubbornly blocked the expression of others.

The reaction of many modern Biblical theologians to this problem has been to reject all ontologies. Sensing the inadequacies of much current doctrine they have invoked a curse upon all ontologies, be they Hellenistic or Germanic in origins, in the name of the living God of Scripture. But this is to forget the basic and inevitable role ontological presuppositions play in the attempt to make the Biblical faith intelligible. It is also to overlook the creative possibilities in ontologies other than the Greek or the idealistic. It is simply a fallacy to argue from the inadequacies of some ontologies to the rejection of all ontologies. Rather, what is indicated is the investigation of ontological patterns that are in fuller harmony with the Biblical witness to God. The problem is one of finding generally intelligible descriptions of reality by which the Biblical picture of God can be interpreted. In an approach to this problem from the standpoint of the kenotic motif as formulated in Scripture, there are two features required of such an ontology. It must be personalistic and dynamic in character. It must give the same ultimacy to personal existence as does Scripture. It must also be able to comprehend change and development as part of the nature of things.

Before we proceed to the doctrine of God, it is necessary to state in general terms the features of an ontology that is personalistic and dynamic. What is a personalistic ontology? In such an ontology what meaning is to be given to such terms as " perfect " or " absolute "? Can such terms be defined as to include the notion of change or growth in the divine life?

The term " personalism " is used here in its broadest sense. It does not imply any of the particular personalistic philosophies formulated in modern times. Rather, reference is made to the basic assumption of personality as the key to ultimate reality. Personalism is the belief that self-determining, creative personal being is the highest order of reality. In contrast to personalism, other ontologies have given ultimacy to some form of reality that they hold transcends personhood. The nonpersonalistic ontologies have given to " being " or the " unconditioned ground of existence " the distinction of having the greatest reality. Hence, they have viewed personal existence as in some sense a limited or inferior form of existence. When such nonpersonalistic ontologies have been applied to the Biblical picture of God, confusion has resulted. These ontologies have been used to interpret a personalistic picture of God in terms which give ultimacy to the impersonal. For this reason, persuasive argument can be made for the use of personalistic patterns of thought for describing the Christian doctrine of God. It would render more intelligible the free, creative change implicit in such notions as divine self-limitation. Personalism has a greater congruity with Biblical modes of thought than the traditional ontologies.

Forsyth recognized this and experimented with reformulations of doctrine in personalistic forms. Basic to his method was the use of analogies drawn from human experience as a means of illumining the being and action of God. His use of personal analogy and anecdote in the treatment of kenosis is an example. However, he was never able to give full or systematic statement to his work in this area. Certainly part of his difficulty stemmed from a danger to which all personalism is heir. This is the difficulty of drawing conclusive analogies from human personality for understanding God. If man is believed to be finite and sinful and God infinite and holy, all such analogies are bound to be limited and finally unsatisfactory. Human personality can be a guide, but it can also be the source of distortion and error. For this reason, Forsyth's Biblical personalism remained inconclusive.

Barth seeks to carry forward the development of a Biblical personalism by overcoming this basic difficulty. He argues that the application of human analogies to God is wrong. It is a lapsing back into " natural theology." He proposes to view the analogy in just the opposite way. God is the supreme person. Men are persons only in a limited or derived sense. We find the true meaning of personhood in God. Men can be spoken of as persons only in the degree to which they reflect the personhood of God. For Barth the word " person " is not a predicate we add to the word " God " to understand it better. Rather, as we come to know God through his self-revelation, we come to know the meaning of person.

The approach Barth suggests is certainly an appealing one in many regards. But it is beset with one very practical difficulty. Just how does one come to think about personality without thinking first about human personality? Certainly the Bible does not teach a theory of divine personality. Rather, we are bound to think in terms that already have meaning for us, even if we transform these terms in thinking about them. The really live alternative for building a Biblical personalism lies in the direction of a dialogue between our understanding of human personality and our understanding of God's action in revelation. Biblical personalism has two points of reference by which to shape its doctrine. It will utilize those insights into personality opened to us in human experience. These insights will then be corrected and reshaped in the light of God's self-revelation.

The analogy from personality works in two directions. It moves from man to God and from God to man. What we know about human personality is used in understanding the personality of God. Such a starting point is inevitable because we are humans. But what God reveals about himself reshapes all we mean when we use the word "person." Our understanding of personality is to be transformed by what the supreme Person reveals about himself. Out of this dialogue can emerge guidelines for building a doctrine of God.

One other major difficulty was encountered in the Greek philosophical ontology and the traditional church doctrine that derives from it. This is the problem of envisaging change or development as part of the divine being. The problem is how to conceive the perfection of God properly. How can God be pictured as the perfect or supreme Being and yet opened to change and growth? In traditional church doctrine, God's existence is eternal, infinite, and unchangeable. By contrast the existence of man and the world is limited and mortal. God is not frustrated in his purposes by any weakness. He is motivated by no lack or want. The basic way in which these perfections were described was dominated by the idea of God as pure being. On these grounds, for the being of God to be eternal, it had to be unchangeable. For God to be unchangeable, he had to be complete in himself. His eternal and independent character was explained in terms of pure, changeless being. God was understood as the *Summum Bonum* or the *Ens Realissimum*.

The problem with this description of God's being is that it is based on static metaphors. The key contrast between God and man is that between the changeless and the changing. Such metaphors are useful in describing the divine unity and immutability. But they do not provide a means for explaining the relatedness of God. They cannot comprehend the interaction between God and man. The drama of salvation, as pictured in the Bible, is one of God's dynamic interactions with men. God responds to man as well as man responds to God. This aspect of Biblical thought, of which kenosis is the supreme example, cannot be understood through static metaphors. The use of such metaphors always ends in having the possibility of God's actions denied by his perfections.

What is needed is a means for describing the eternal, independent existence of God which also comprehends his relatedness and limitation. The key to this problem lies in a closer analysis of such terms as " perfect " and " absolute " when applied to God. As these terms are applied to God traditionally, they imply that God is a being in all respects absolutely perfect and unsurpassable. God is in no respect surpassable or perfectible by anyone including himself. The outcome of this use of terms is obvious and unsatisfactory. Yet there is another way of conceiving the perfection of God.

God can be conceived as being absolutely perfect or unsurpassable in some respects, while being only potentially perfect in others. This means that while God is perfect in certain respects, he is open to growth or development in other aspects of his being. Specifically, in Christian doctrine God is perfect in respect to his love. The will of love for the salvation of man is an unswerving or unchangeable quality in the divine life. But by contrast, God is only potentially perfect or unsurpassable when considered in his relationship to creation. There is a quality of openness or freedom in God's relation to men and the world. In creation, God accepted the limitation of co-existence with man and the world, which have their own creativity and freedom. Hence, as long as there is a real human history in which men are acting freely, and as long as God is concerned with men, there is some aspect of the divine being that is only potentially perfect. If God has a relationship with creation, and the created order has some measure of freedom, then there is an element of openness or incompleteness in the divine being.

Against such an analysis of the divine being the defenders of traditional theology have objected strongly. They claim it leads to belief in a finite God who is powerless to ensure the salvation of man and the world. To say God is in any sense incomplete is to make him impotent. The heart of the traditional argument for the absolute perfection of God in all respects is the belief that any measure of incompleteness implies impotence. But is such a contention sound? Incompleteness does not necessarily imply impotence. It is equally conceivable that incompleteness is simply a temporary stage in a developmental process which will ultimately be perfect. Within such a conception of the divine being, God can be said to be absolute because incompleteness does not have the final word. The divine being will be completed in conformity with God's will of love. The perfection of God lies in the fact that what he will become is not a denial of his present nature. God's involvement in historical process enriches but does not distort his being.

The definition of God's being in dynamic terms involves viewing the divine being in two aspects: (1) God can be said to be already perfect or unsurpassable in some aspects of his being. Specifically, in Christian doctrine God is unsurpassable in his will of love for men. (2) Because of his involvement with history, God's being can be said to be only potentially complete in some aspects. The ultimate completion of his being is involved in temporal processes. By this twofold approach to the divine being it is possible to envisage both the permanence and the change that are basic to the Biblical picture of God. Within this general ontological pattern expression can be given to the limitation and concrete involvement of God in the life of man and the world.

The Doctrine of God

Theology reaches an ultimate embarrassment when it comes to the doctrine of God. Every attempt to treat the doctrine is haunted by the realization that its subject matter is by definition beyond the power of human words. The possibility of speaking about God is grounded on the assumption that God has revealed himself. Hence, in line with our methodology the doctrine is to be built by relating the Biblical witness to revelation to those personalistic, dynamic interpretations of reality current in the modern world. What is undertaken here is not a complete account of the doctrine. Rather, concern is to be centered in those aspects of it illumined by the kenotic motif. What does kenosis tell of the action and being of God? How can the doctrine of God be formulated so as to make kenosis intelligible?

Basic to the Christian doctrine of God is the affirmation of God's reality in terms of his love. This affirmation can be stated formally: "God is that Being, made known in his self-revelation, who loves in freedom." The key to God's being is his freedom to love and his sovereign freedom in loving. The consideration of God's love and his freedom cannot be separated from one another. God's love must not be thought out of relation to his freedom, else it becomes grasping desire, not love. To say "God loves in freedom" means God is free to love. He does not love out of any need. His love for others is not initially a way of completing his incompleteness. Similarly, God's freedom must not be thought out of relation to his love, else it becomes sheer caprice. To say "God loves in freedom" means God is free to act in any way to fulfill his will of love. The freedom of God is not arbitrary freedom. It is freedom to fulfill his will of love for man and the world. God's love is the supreme determinant of the divine action. And his acts are always free. Only by thinking

of these qualities in relation to one another can a proper understanding of God be reached.

What is the most basic implication of the statement "God
loves in freedom"? Fundamentally, love implies a relation to
another. Love means fellowship and, hence, the existence of
someone else who can be the object of love. Because the divine
love is a free, sovereign love, it is not bound to love someone or
something that coexists with it. The divine love is free to create
its own object of love. The creation of an object for God's love
is affirmed in saying he is the Creator of all things. Creation is
the first expression of God's love. In creating man and the world,
God has the objects of his love through which it reaches its
highest expression. Through creation God enters a relationship
with something other than himself. He is related to man and the
world in love. This relationship has two main characteristics
which reveal important aspects of the nature of God.

First, the relation of God to his creation implies limitation.
To say man and the world exist in distinction from God implies
they are a limit upon him. Creation means the existence of
something that is not God and is, hence, in some measure, a
limitation upon God. To be sure, this is a limitation which has
been freely accepted, since God chose to create the world. God
is not limited by something that coexisted eternally with him.
The limitation upon God brought about by creation is a free
self-limitation. It is, in other words, a kenosis. In creation God
has freely accepted limitation in the fulfillment of his will for
love or fellowship with another.

The point at which the created order becomes a limitation
upon God is not in its mere physical existence. The existence
of a universe of matter and energy created by God would not
necessarily limit him. It is quite conceivable that such a body of
matter and energy could be so completely under the control of
God as to be identical with him. The created order becomes a
limit upon God inasmuch as it has a free and independent existence of its own. The created order is not simply a divinely
wound clock running according to a fully predetermined plan.

It has sources of creativity and freedom within itself. The emergence of novelty in nature and supremely the emergence of freedom in man witness to this. It is the creation of man and a world with limited, but none the less real, freedom that constitutes a self-imposed limitation upon God. In its primary expression through creation the divine love has a kenotic quality. It is a love that expresses itself uniquely by an act of self-limitation.

Secondly, the relation of God to creation is personal, not mechanical. God could exist in such a relation to man and the world as to determine fully every event at every moment. But this would mean no real freedom for man, nor any novelty in the history of the world. Such a relation would be mechanical. God would appear, as he does in some of the cruder forms of theism, as the Cosmic Kingpin of a great clockwork in which man is just an interesting cog. Such a mechanistic doctrine may assure the omnipotence of God, but it does so at the price of vitiating his love and man's freedom. Actually, a far more subtle model is needed to comprehend the relation of God and the world. A closer illustration comes from the relations of persons to one another. This is the type of relation illustrated in the Biblical drama of God's seeking and saving love for mankind.

To comprehend the uniquely personal quality of God's relation to the created order it is necessary to remember creation does not stand in a perfect relation to God. It is his creation. But it is a fallen creation. Through man's misuse of his freedom, creation is alienated from its Creator. It stands in enmity to him. God could overcome this alienation by doing away with freedom. This he does not do. Instead, God seeks to create a new fellowship with men through forgiveness and renewal. The new fellowship that God intends for men fulfills their personality. Man becomes through salvation not an automaton but a full man. The relation between God and man is fully personal.

The history of Biblical religion shows that while God's will of love for man is constant, it is expressed in various ways. The Biblical history of salvation is one of changing stratagems in

God's search for men. The very division of Scripture into Old Covenant and New Covenant witnesses to this. The religion of Israel and the religion of the church represent differing stratagems in God's search for man. Yet one God is revealed through both. God fulfills his will of love in ways appropriate to the concrete situation in which men then live. It is for this reason that Biblical religion can be understood in terms of a history of salvation. The expression of God's will for the salvation of mankind is made in relation to the historical situation of mankind. There is, as Barth so aptly puts it, "a holy mutability" about God. God does not make simply one approach to man but many. His actions in human history have been both judgment and redemption. God has spoken through law and prophets, wisdom literature, and poetry. He has acted in the history of his people. He has finally spoken in the person of his Son. Yet there lies behind all these varied actions the love of God for his creation. The acts of God in salvation can only be understood as personal acts.

What does it mean to speak of God and the fulfillment of his purposes in personal terms? Inasmuch as a person is a self-initiating center of his own activity, he is capable of responsive change in the fulfillment of his will. A person is not limited to a predetermined plan. He is capable of responding to the infinite variety of concrete situations that he experiences. A full, well-integrated person is possessed of what psychologists call "ego-strength." This refers to the person's ability to stay integrated in the fulfillment of his basic goals or purposes. A person who is mature can respond creatively to the myriad world of external reality. He is able to relate the new and changing in experience to certain overarching goals. A full personal being can be said to possess the capacity for infinite, responsive change in relation to basic goals or purposes.

Needless to say, human personality does not work completely on this model. Human personality is incomplete and fragmentary. The capacity of a finite personality to change remains finite. And his goals weaken and change. Yet this model from human personality does illumine God's being and action as witnessed to by Scripture. The various stratagems taken by God in his relation to men reveal the divine capacity for infinite responsive change. In the fulfillment of his will for loving fellowship with men, God responds in a variety of ways to man in his concrete historical situation. There is at the heart of the divine being the capacity for infinite responsive change in the interest of a fixed purpose. The fixed purpose is God's will of love for his creation. The infinite responsive change comes through God's relation to men and the world.

If the being of God is defined in terms of his capacity for infinite responsive change in the light of a constant purpose, then a new definition of divine absoluteness is possible. The absoluteness of God is his unlimited capacity for relating to men and the world in the service of his unchanging purpose of love. By contrast, man has only a limited capacity for change. In his relation to the world of reality about him man sometimes reacts inappropriately. And in the process of interaction man often compromises or corrupts his initial purposes. By contrast God's absoluteness lies in his capacity for entirely appropriate relations to the created order and an entirely unswerving purpose. To carry along the psychological analogy, God could be said to have unlimited " ego-strength." His selfhood remains unimpaired no matter how deeply and intimately he becomes involved in others. It is this capacity which sets God's person above that of man.

From this perspective it is possible to interpret the kenosis revealed in Christ. The coming of Christ was the ultimate stratagem of God's love for his creation. As the writer to the Hebrews put it: " In many and various ways God spoke of old to our fathers by the prophets; but in these last days he has spoken to us by a Son." (Heb. 1:1-2.) God has undertaken to speak to men as a man. God did not merely address man through the words of men. God was personally present as a man himself. This is the meaning of incarnation. It reveals God's personal identification with the world of men he seeks to save. The revelation of

God lost any quality of indirectness with the coming of Christ. He is God personally present in his creation. Yet at the same time he is a man. How is this possible? Only through a change in the divine life. This change is a self-limitation in which God surrenders the complete freedom of his transcendent life to come into bondage to the powers of sin and death, which are part and parcel of creaturely existence. God sets aside the infinitude of life within himself to take up life within the confines of creaturely existence.

The self-emptying of God in Christ is the stratagem by which God speaks his saving word to men as a man. The classical problem posed by this kenosis is, How can God accept the limitations of humanity upon himself and still remain God? Traditionally, the answer to this has been sought in finding how the presence of God in Christ was scaled down to a point where it did not vitiate the reality of his humanity. But to look in this direction for the answer is to overlook certain important factors.

First, God is already in a self-limiting relation with the whole of the created order. A self-limiting relation to man and the world is not a unique event in the life of God; it is a basic quality of his life. Kenosis is not something that just happened once in Christ; it is something that has marked the whole history of God's dealing with men. The kenosis in Christ is the ultimate expression of God's kenotic love for man, but it is not an example isolated from the rest.

Secondly, to say God has become incarnate in the life of a particular man does not mean God has entered a realm foreign to himself. Human finitude, as such, does not exclude God from it. Man excludes God from his life through sin, not finitude. So, the limitations of man — mortality, ignorance, and want — do not of themselves alienate man from God. God's intimate, responsive relation to the world witnesses to the fact that this is his world. The uniquely full relation between God and man seen in Christ is grounded in God's initial relation to all mankind. Kenosis means there is a manward movement in the divine life that is expressed in creation and finally consummated in in-carnation.

Thirdly, kenosis is the highest expression of the divine ab-soluteness. Thomasius perceived this in his oft-repeated formula: "Self-limitation is self-determination." He argued from the grounds that self-determination is the highest expression of per-sonal life. The highest personal freedom is the freedom of com-plete self-determination. If self-determination is to be complete, it must include the power to accept limitation. Hence, the self-limitation of God in Christ is the vindication of God's self-determining power. Limitation is not the embarrassment of the divine power and absoluteness, but in reality its highest ex-pression. The question that arises is just how this seemingly paradoxical assertion can be vindicated. Thomasius and the mediating theologians with him tried to do this by predicating certain changes among the members of the Trinity to make self-limitation possible. Such attempts were foredoomed to failure. The creative possibility lies rather in a thorough redefinition of the divine absoluteness in dynamic terms.

To understand kenosis as the highest expression of the divine absoluteness it is necessary to determine its purpose. The pur-pose of the divine self-limitation in Christ is the salvation of mankind. Incarnation is God's supreme stratagem in his search for sinful man. In the incarnation the last barrier between God and man is removed, and man is saved by sharing the life of God. In other words, kenosis is the expression of the eternal, divine will of love for mankind. It serves God's unchangeable will of love by allowing him to enter fully the world of change-able human beings for their salvation. Now, if the absoluteness of God is in his unlimited capacity for fulfilling his will of love through relations with the created order, then kenosis is the supreme expression of this capacity. Kenosis is the highest ex-pression of the divine freedom because it is the means of God fulfilling his will of love for man.

There is still another aspect to the divine kenosis than those revealed in creation and incarnation. This is the divine kenosis in human history. The whole of human existence represents a continuation of the act of self-limitation seen in creation and redemption. For inasmuch as human history is a realm of finite but real freedom, it represents a limitation upon the divine life. The very possibility of human history's being more than the bleak repetition of mechanical patterns is the existence of significant freedom in human affairs. Such freedom means that to a certain degree the future of mankind is still open. The future is not completely contained in the present or the past. The problem that arises is, Just how does this kind of freedom affect God? Certainly one possibility is to say such freedom has no relation to God. God is not concerned with human history. He is beyond the changes that mark all human affairs. Christian faith rejects this possibility with its confession that God is Lord of all. Human history with its freedom and change is within God's purpose of love. These two assertions about human history — its freedom and God's concern for it — can only be related in terms of kenosis. God has freely accepted the limitation of granting to man freedom in his history. Yet at the same time God is involved in history, seeking the redemption of mankind.

This kenotic understanding of God's relation to history leads to a new understanding of the divine being. If God is involved in human history — the realm of change and incompleteness — then God is in some measure subject to change and incompleteness. God's interaction with the world is partly determinative of his being. If the divine personality is defined in terms of responsive change, as has been done, then it implies God is affected by the human deeds to which he responds. In this light it is possible to make sense of those Biblical expressions about God's anger, his sorrow, his joy, or his zeal. These are ways of describing God's personal relations with men. Biblical religion is based on the faith that when man responds to God he is not responding to a changeless, impersonal It. Rather, he is interacting with the supreme Person. And as in any truly personal relation, there is change in both parties. Such responsive interaction with men is possible because God has limited himself.

Strong objection has been taken to this position on the grounds that it endangers God's absoluteness. It is argued that to make God in any way dependent on the world is to open the possibility of God's being overcome by the world. But such objections overlook the precise terms in which God's limitations were described. God is determined in part by his interaction with the world. God is also partly determined by his unchanging will of love for the salvation of men. God's being represents an interaction between these two factors. The divine absoluteness was defined in this light as the ultimate triumph of his unchanging will of love. God is absolute by virtue of the fact that his unchanging will of love is never finally distorted, corrupted, or frustrated by his interaction with the world. The power of God ultimately ensures the salvation of the world. But the key word here is " ultimately." This means that at any given moment in human history God's being is incomplete because of his relation to mankind. God has freely accepted temporary incompleteness in the interest of open personal relations with his creatures. This incompleteness is to be completed by God's relation to men in the fulfillment of his will of love.

The history of salvation is the drama of the relation of God and man. It is a drama marked by temporary frustrations and incompleteness, for human history is the realm of sin and death. It is a drama whose inevitable outcome is within the loving purpose of God. But it is a drama whose exact course is not yet marked out.

In the light of this understanding of the incompleteness of the divine being, it becomes possible to bring into focus an aspect of the kenotic motif often overlooked. This is the theme of exaltation of the Christ, which is basic to the kenotic motif in the New Testament. In the Philippian hymn, the Christ is granted the new and higher status of Lord through an exaltation. Despite the centrality of this exaltation in the New Testament, most kenotic doctrine has been strangely one-sided. Emphasis has always been placed on the divine self-limitation without reference to the subsequent exaltation. Such an omission was inevitable in the light of the traditional doctrine of God as changeless being. Within that framework any idea of growth or development of God was unthinkable. Yet this is what the kenotic motif clearly implies. Because of his free sharing in human life, even to the point of sharing death, the Christ was granted a new and higher status than he had in his preexistent state. Through a relation with mankind the divine being was enriched.

Biblical religion sees this completion of the divine being in eschatological terms. The Bible points to a consummation of history in which the brokenness, sin, and death of this present age are at an end. At the consummation the Lordship of God over all is complete and all power and dominion come into his hands. (For example, see I Cor. 15:24-28.) This is the triumph of God's will of love for his creation.

The present age is the age of the divine humiliation or kenosis. God has limited himself, giving to men a freedom that they misused. This present age of divine limitation looks forward to a time of completion. It is possible to look forward in hope to the exaltation of the divine Lordship over all because this triumph was prefigured in the resurrection-ascension of Christ. The exaltation of Christ is an anticipatory event. It is the promise of that completion of the divine Lordship at the end of history. Until that time of completion, God shares in the incompleteness and sufferings of this present age.

This incompleteness is real within the life of God, but it does not frustrate the eventual triumph of his love. God's suffering of the incompleteness and sin of man is a suffering freely accepted. In this sense it can be called kenotic suffering. It is suffering freely accepted in order to overcome it. Because of his involvement in the history of the world, God shares the sin and suffering of this world, not as their victim but as Redeemer. Biblical religion knows nothing of a finite God who is a victim of this world. Rather, it speaks of God as freely and fully involved in the world, yet through this involvement he is triumphing over the world.

Kenosis is the characteristic of God's being and action in every aspect. God the Father is Creator by virtue of accepting the limitation of his creation. God the Son is Redeemer in accepting the limitations of the humanity he seeks to save. God the Spirit is the Perfecter of man by living in and through his history and accepting his suffering. Kenosis is not an event in the life of the Trinity as the mediating theologians pictured it. Nor does it become possible because of certain rearrangements of persons or attributes in the Trinity. Kenosis is a characteristic action of the divine love as it seeks and creates fellowship with men and the world. Kenosis is the key to the saving action of God. His characteristic act in salvation is not one of self-assertion but rather of self-negation. In contrast to all human attempts at self-salvation, God saves in a gesture of radical self-giving. God limits himself, taking upon himself the incompleteness, brokenness, and sin that separate men from him. Free self-limitation is the characteristic of God's every act, indeed, of God's own person.

The Man Christ Jesus

With the advent of the modern religious consciousness in the nineteenth century, Christological thinking increasingly focused on the question of Jesus' consciousness. Questions were asked about Jesus' moral and spiritual life and its development. How did Jesus' unique being as both human and divine affect his mental processes? Did his consciousness of God and the world undergo a normal growth? Interest was high over the question of Jesus' so-called " messianic consciousness." What was Jesus' understanding of his own mission? Was it possible for him to know himself to be the Savior of the world? These and a flood of similar questions occupied the attention of a whole generation of New Testament scholars. Yet instead of these questions finding answers, they simply begot more questions until thought on this subject was stymied. Such a result was inevitable. For in certain respects the question of Jesus' consciousness is unanswerable. On purely historical grounds it is impossible to reconstruct the mental processes of a person, especially when our knowledge of him is based on only fragmentary written records. The New Testament itself witnesses only in the most indirect manner to Jesus' self-consciousness. Only the most limited assertions can be made about this difficult subject.

Although the form given this question in the nineteenth century was misleading, it is a question of profound significance. It posed in the sharpest possible way the question of Jesus' humanity. The fully human character of Jesus' bodily functioning had been established in the anti-Gnostic controversies in the early centuries of the church's life. It remained until modern times for the question of Jesus' humanity to be asked in its most acute form. This is the question whether Jesus' mental and spiritual functioning was fully human. To say that God has become man must include his mental and emotional life. The evidence of the New Testament, although fragmentary, does indicate that Jesus had limited knowledge. He shared fully in the historical and scientific views of his day, even when they were in error. Jesus thought and acted as a man of his time.

However, assuming full humanity for Jesus' mental and spiritual life leaves the problem of describing his divinity in its most difficult form. In much traditional Christology, Jesus' humanity consisted mainly in his bodily functions. His mental functioning was controlled by the Logos and was characterized potentially, if not actually, by omniscience. In this way a means was provided for explaining how he could be both human and divine. If it is claimed that Jesus had fully human mental functionings, how can he be designated as divine? Would it not be, as the critics of kenotic Christology have always claimed, that loss of divine consciousness means loss of divine being?

A kenotic Christology follows two lines of thought in dealing with the question of Christ's divinity: his divinity is to be described in terms of God's freedom and in terms of Christ's saving power.

The kenotic motif expresses in its most radical form the freedom of God. God is free in the fulfillment of his eternal purpose of love for man. In God's becoming a particular man with a fully human consciousness, his freedom reaches its highest expression. To use Barth's apt saying: God is free to become, as it were, "God for us a second time" in becoming the man Jesus. In becoming a true man, God does not cease being God. In becoming a man, God is expressing in a unique way his Lordship over the created order. He expresses his love by entering fully into his created order as a particular man. But in doing this, he still remains fully God. Traditional theology has always tended to hedge in making this sort of an assertion because of its belief that the finite was not capable of bearing the infinite. God, the Infinite, was by definition incapable of incorporation into a finite human life. So the divine nature of Christ was always kept scrupulously separated from his human nature. The Infinite would inevitably overpower the finite if they were brought into full contact with one another. This position was generally taken by the upholders of traditional theology, the Calvinists particularly, in the interest of protecting the deity of God and the humanity of man. But it did this by holding them in separation from one another.

The assertion of the freedom of God means God is free to transform his mode of existence from the infinite to the finite. This freedom means God and man do not stand in radical opposition to one another. They are related as Creator and creature. The Creator is free to share fully the life of his creature. It is a life that is not foreign to him. There is a humanity about God. His being has its manward side. Certainly it is this to which the mythological picture of a preexistent Christ in the "form of God" points. As New Testament study has shown, the Christ was already in his preexistent state a Man; yet he was a Man sharing the realm of God. He was a Man dwelling "in the form of God" who then came to share the "form of a servant." The radical distinction between finite and infinite was unknown in the New Testament. By kenosis God is simply expressing his Lordship over creation in entering it.

The freedom of God is a basic quality of the divine being. It is not a characteristic that can be explained in terms of something else within the divine life. It is, rather, this radical freedom which constitutes God as God. God is free to be Lord of all. So he is free to transform his mode of existence without becoming unlike himself. To say God is free means we can confess him as Lord even in the form of a suffering, dying man. He is Lord as much on the cross as in the glory of his transcendent life. This radical freedom of God revealed in Christ is not something that thought can explain. It cannot be rationalized. It is the characteristic of God that makes him God. It is a characteristic most clearly perceived in the person of Christ.

Kenotic Christology also approaches the question of Christ's divinity in terms of his saving power. If the divinity of Christ is not expressed in terms of some changeless residuum of divinity, of what, then, does it consist? Or, to put the question in another form: If the Christ is a man, how is he different from other men? By virtue of what, can he be said to be divine? Christ is divine by virtue of being God's unique agent for the redemption of mankind. Christ's divinity lies in his power to save. He is the source of transforming power that issues in new life. Jesus Christ is the one through whom God creates new fellowship with men who have been alienated from him by their sin. This line of approach to the question of Christ's divinity is certainly indicated by Paul. To the Corinthians he speaks of God's presence in Christ in terms of his reconciling work.

Therefore, if any one is in Christ, he is a new creation; the old has passed away, behold, the new has come. All this is from God, who through Christ reconciled us to himself and gave us the ministry of reconciliation; that is, God was in Christ reconciling the world to himself. (II Cor. 5:17-19.)

The divinity of Christ is not described in terms of static divine being but divine reconciling activity. "God was in Christ reconciling the world to himself." The description of Christ's divinity follows from this as if by logical argument. When by faith a man "is in Christ, he is a new creation." The only way in which he can become a new creation is by virtue of having met God the Creator. Men have met their Creator afresh in the person of

Christ. It is for this reason Christians confess him as divine. The man Jesus of Nazareth, without ceasing to be fully human, is the Agent of God's redemptive work. In him, God has accepted the servant form. Yet it is God who is still Redeemer even as he lives and acts through this human life. The one who was " in the form of God " took the " form of a servant " so men could know him as Lord and Savior.

Epilogue

No contemporary theological statement can be considered complete without at least some consideration of its implications for the ecumenical movement. Certainly no issue is more basic in this regard than that of Christology. In particular the problem faced in ecumenical conversation has focused on the question of how the Christology of the great Creeds and confessional statements is to relate to the contemporary proclamation of Christ. This problem is vexed enough when considered within Protestantism alone, but when the scope of concern is widened to include the churches of Orthodoxy and Roman Catholicism, the problem becomes a cardinal one that presents no foreseeable solutions. The churches of the Catholic traditions, and with them conservative Protestantism, have insisted that Christology can be reconsidered only within the framework of Athanasian orthodoxy as given creedal authority in Nicaea and Chalcedon. The patristic formulation of the doctrine of the Trinity and of Christ's two natures has an authority that cannot be challenged in any reconstructive effort. True, wide latitude has often been given, particularly within Orthodoxy, to the interpretation of the Chalcedonian formulas. Yet for the majority of the churches of Christendom these formulas have a statutory and living place that will not be compromised by them for fear of compromising the faith itself.

By contrast, a very different attitude has been taken to these formulas in this rethinking of the kenotic Christology. While the epoch-making importance of these formulas in their time and their value as a link with the faith of the past is recognized, their inadequacies have been carefully scrutinized. One of the grounds for the reconstruction of the doctrine of God was the rejection of the ontology within which these creeds were formulated. Does this imply a rejection of these creeds and with it the rejection of closer fellowship with the communions that value them so highly? The answer is, No, such is not necessarily the case. The justification of such an answer calls for several observations about the place of creedal orthodoxy in the life of the church.

In the first place, it should be noted that the reconstruction of the kenosis doctrine undertaken here was only in part an attempt at modernization. This restatement was in part an attempt to go back and read the Biblical witness in terms of itself. The negative judgment made here about the adequacy of the patristic Christology was made only in part because of its incongruity with modern thought. The great creeds of Christendom are not to be overthrown simply because of their clash with modernity. The more important point at which creedal orthodoxy came in for negative judgment was its inability to express the Biblical faith. The fact of doctrinal development is denied by no responsible churchman today. The Christianity of the New Testament is not the same as the Christianity of the fourth and fifth centuries. The doctrinal development witnessed to by the ecumenical creeds represents, in part, a continuation and, in part, a denial of the doctrine of the first century. The mind of the church was occupied with questions in the age of Chalcedon far different from those in the age of Nero. An inevitable selection had been made of certain elements from the fullness of revelation in Christ to which unique emphasis was given. Such a selection led to an inevitable distortion. The struggle against the great heresies of the day had left its marks on the mind of the church. In formulating protective doctrines, the church had overlooked much that was basic to the New Testament faith.

Recognizing this distortion, appeal has been made afresh to the earliest witness to revelation — the New Testament.

Secondly, rejecting the ontology within which the creeds were formulated does not imply rejecting the content of the creeds themselves. Creedal statements take shape through a language that bears the impress of its time. In this regard they are documents limited in value to that time when their language forms were intelligible. Yet their function is to bear witness to a faith that transcends all its formulations. The faith and its creedal formulations are not identical. So it is possible to exercise the critical faculties to the full regarding the language forms of the past while still holding to the faith to which they point.

Thirdly, much of the exception taken to creedal orthodoxy has been in regard to questions where it has been misapplied. When any doctrinal formula is approached, care must be taken to determine what it does and does not talk about. Such care has seldom been taken with the creedal formulas. These formulas were in the first instance fashioned to deal with certain heresies about Christ's person. These heresies and the church's answer to them were formulated in essentially ontological terms. They described how the divine and human natures received concrete individualization in the person of Christ. Within the intellectual setting provided by the Hellenistic world, these formulas were invaluable guides to the faith; but when these same formulas are applied to problems raised by the modern psychological and historical conception of personality, confusion is twice confounded. Yet this has been precisely what has been happening since the advent of the mediating theology of the last century. People have been seeking answers to essentially psychological and historical questions about Jesus' self-conscious or his mental and spiritual growth from creedal formulas that originally were never meant to deal with such questions. No amount of respect for creedal orthodoxy should lead us to seek in it what was never there.

In the growing ecumenical conversation of the future, the

question of creedal orthodoxy and contemporary restatements of Christology will have a central place. In such conversation two attitudes must be avoided. Men must not be tempted to submerge real differences or to lay aside the historical method in the hope that we can purchase some measure of unity through a merely verbal acceptance of the words and formulas of the past. Men must not be tempted, either, to dispose of these statements as if they were mere historical curios that no longer speak to us. Instead, we must understand creedal orthodoxy of the past in the light of history. We must see them as witnesses, often as great and good witnesses, yet also fallible human witnesses, to the one Lord Jesus Christ. Only in this way can we move closer to discovering the oneness we have in him.

Notes

1. Frederich Loofs, "Kenosis," *Encyclopedia of Religion and Ethics*, ed. by James Hastings (Charles Scribner's Sons, 1915), Vol. VII, p. 683.
2. A necessity faced in writing a book like this is choosing a suitable name for that branch of philosophy which deals with the structures of being. The traditional title "metaphysics" seems inadequate because it suggests only structures beyond or outside those known in the natural world. Hence, I have settled on the term "ontology" because it is a more inclusive term. Throughout, this term is used to characterize the structure of being as found in God and in the natural world. The term implies no single theory of being. It is used to characterize the various theories of being encountered throughout the history of the kenosis motif.
3. H. R. Mackintosh, *The Doctrine of the Person of Jesus Christ* (Charles Scribner's Sons, 1912), p. 466.
4. *Calvin: Institutes of the Christian Religion*, ed. by John T. McNeill; tr. and indexed by Ford Lewis Battles, The Library of Christian Classics (The Westminster Press, 1959), II. xiii. 2.
5. Ernst Lohmeyer, *Die Briefe an die Philipper, an die Kolosser und an Philemon* (Vanderhoeck und Ruprecht, Göttingen, 1930), pp. 90–99. See also for a different approach the article by Jeremias in *Studia Paulina*, ed. by J. N. Sevenester and W. C. van Unnick (De Erven F. Bohn N. V., Haarlem, 1953), pp. 152–154.
6. Ernst Barnikol, *Philipper 2: Der Marcionitische Ursprung des Mythos-Satzes Phil. 2, 6-7* (Walter G. Muhlau, Kiel, 1932).

7. Joseph B. Lightfoot, *Saint Paul's Epistle to the Philippians* (The Macmillan Company, London, 1879), pp. 127–137.

8. Johonnaes Behm, "*Morphē*," *Theologisches Wörterbuch zum Neuen Testament*, ed. by Gerhard Kittel (W. Kohlhammer, Stuttgart, 1933), Vol. 4, pp. 751 ff. Another important, and in many ways contrasting, lexical study is found in J. H. Moulton and G. Milligan, *The Vocabulary of the Greek Testament* (Hodder & Stoughton, Ltd., London, 1924), Part V, p. 417.

9. Cullmann gives an extended treatment of the Heavenly Man idea in Jewish literature in his *Christology of the New Testament* (The Westminster Press, 1959). The place of this theme in Hellenistic-Gnostic literature and its importance for the New Testament is described by Ernst Käsemann in an article, "Kritische Analyse von Phil. 2.5-11," *Zeitschrift für Theologie und Kirche* (Vol. 47, 1950), pp. 313 ff.

10. The translation of this passage is quoted from Charles E. Raven, *Apollinarianism* (Cambridge University Press, 1923), p. 203.

11. This is from Apollinarius' commentary on John's Gospel quoted from Raven, *op. cit.*, p. 205.

12. Bernard of Clairvaux, *Sermons on Various Subjects*, LX. 1. See also "On the Ascension of Lucifer and Adam, Fourth Sermon for the Feast of the Ascension" and "First Sermon for Advent: On the Coming of Christ." *St. Bernard's Sermons*, tr. by a Priest of Mount Melleray (The Carroll Press, 1950), Vols. I and II.

13. Bernard of Clairvaux, *Sermons on the Song of Songs*, XI. 7, *Life and Works of St. Bernard*, ed. by Dom John Mabillion (John Hodges, London, 1896), Vol. IV, p. 59.

14. Martin Luther, *Werke* (Herman Böhlaus, Weimar, 1927), XVII, 2, pp. 238–239.

15. *Ibid.*

16. *Ibid.*, X, 1, pp. 62–63.

17. *Ibid.*, X, 1, p. 63.

18. *Calvin: Institutes*, II. xiii. 1.

19. *Ibid.*, II. xiv. 2.

20. *Ibid.*, II. xiii. 4.

21. Martin Luther, *Sammtliche Werke* (Carl Hender, Erlangen, 1841), 30, pp. 62–67.

22. Martinum Chemnicium, *De Duabus Naturis in Christo* (Ex Officina Donati Ritzenhaini, Jena, 1570), pp. 24–25.

23. Johannes H. Heideggerus, *Corpus Theologiae*, XIX, 15. The translations of the Reformed theologians are from Heinrich Heppe, *Reformed Dogmatics* (George Allen & Unwin, Ltd., London, 1950).

24. Hieronymi Zanchii, *De Incarnatione Filii Dei*, Bk. i.

25. Leonardus Riisenius, *Francisi Turretini Compendium Theologiae*, XI, 39, 4.

26. Samuelis Maresius, *Collegium Theologicum*, IX, 30.

27. N. L. Graf von Zinzendorf, *Vier und dreyszig Homilae über die Wunden-Litaney der Brüder* . . . (Barby?: 174?), p. 21. See also Zinzendorf, *Ein und zwanzig Discurse über die Augspurgische Confession* . . . (n. p., 174?), pp. 65, 95, 121 ff., and *Naturelle Reflexiones über allerhand Materien* . . . (n. p., 1749?), p. 359.

28. Gottfried Thomasius, "Ein Beitrag zur kirchlichen Christologie," *Zeitschrift für Protestantismus und Kirche* (Neunter Band, 1845).

29. Gottfried Thomasius, *Christi Person und Werk* (Dritte Auflage, Andreas Deichert, Erlangen, 1886), Vol. 1, p. 448.

30. Dorner's criticisms appeared in the second edition of his *Entwicklungsgeschichte*, 1853, and in the *Jahrbüchern für Deutsche Theologie*, 1856. His article in the *Jahrbüchern*, "Über die richtige Fassung des dogmatischen Begriffs der Unveränderlichkeit Gottes," was not only a trenchant criticism of Thomasius but also the basis of a very important restatement of the doctrine of the divine impossibility.

31. The evolution of Thomasius' thought can be traced through the various editions of his *Christi Person und Werk* and his journal articles.

Thomasius, Gottfried, *Beitrag zur kirchlichen Christologie*. Theodor Bläsing, Erlangen, 1845.

—— "Ein Beitrag zur kirchlichen Christologie," *Zeitschrift für Protestantismus und Kirche*, Neue Folge, Neunter Band, G. C. A. Harless, editor. Theodor Bläsing, Erlangen, 1845.

—— *Das Bekenntnis der evangelisch-lutherischen Kirche in der Konsequenz seines Prinzips*. August Recknagel, Nurnberg, 1848.

—— *Christi Person und Werk*. 3 vols. Theodor Bläsing, Erlangen, 1853–1861.

—— *Christi Person und Werk*. Zweite Auflage. 3 vols. Theodor Bläsing, Erlangen, 1856–1863.

—— *Christi Person und Werk.* Dritte Auflage. 2 vols. Andreas Deichert, Erlangen, 1886–1888.

—— "Erwiderung," *Zeitschrift für Protestantismus und Kirche,* Neue Folge, Elfter Band, G. C. A. Harless, editor. Theodor Bläsing, Erlangen, 1846.

32. Thomasius spoke his final word on this question in the last edition of *Christi Person und Werk* on which this section is based.

33. Gess's position is given in two of his books: *Die Lehre von der Person Christi* (Bahmaier's Buchhandlung, Basel, 1856) and *Das Dogma von Christi Person und Werk* (C. Detloff, Basel, 1887), 3 vols.

34. J. H. August Ebrard, *Das Dogma von heiligen Abendmahl* (Heinrich Zimmer, Frankfurt, 1845), Vol. 2, p. 790. For a fuller statement of his position, see his *Christliche Dogmatik* (A. W. Unzer, Königsberg, 1863), 2 vols.

35. H. Martensen, *Christian Dogmatics,* tr. by William Urwick (T. & T. Clark, Edinburgh, 1892).

36. G. W. F. Hegel, *Encyclopedia of Philosophy,* sec. 5, tr. by G. E. Mueller (Philosophical Library, Inc., 1959).

37. *Ibid.,* sec. 11.

38. *Ibid.,* sec. 140.

39. G. W. F. Hegel, *The Phenomenology of Mind,* tr. by J. Baillie (George Allen & Unwin, Ltd., London, 1955), p. 756.

40. *Ibid.,* pp. 762–765.

41. The fullest account of this is in Hegel's treatment of the absolute religion in *Lectures on the Philosophy of Religion,* tr. by E. B. Speers and J. B. Sanderson (Kegan Paul, Trench, Trubner & Co., Ltd., London, 1895), Vols. II and III.

42. Hegel, *Lectures on the Philosophy of Religion,* Vol. III, p. 99.

43. *Ibid.*

44. Theodore A. Liebner, *Christologie oder die christologische Einheit des dogmatischen Systems* (Vanderhoeck und Ruprecht, Göttingen, 1849), p. 319.

45. David Friedrich Strauss, *The Life of Jesus,* tr. from the fourth German edition (Chapman Brothers, London, 1846), Vol. 3, p. 434.

46. H. R. Mackintosh, *Types of Modern Theology* (James Nisbet & Co., Ltd., London, 1937), p. 118.

47. Peter Taylor Forsyth, *The Person and Place of Jesus Christ* (Independent Press, Ltd., London, 1955), pp. 294–295.

48. *Ibid.*
49. Charles Gore, "The Inspiration of Scripture," *Lux Mundi* (12th ed.; John Murray, London, 1891), pp. 249 ff.
50. Forsyth, *op. cit.*, p. 347.
51. *Ibid.*, pp. 282–283.
52. Frederic Godet, *Commentary on the Gospel of John*, tr. by Timothy Dwight (Funk & Wagnalls Company, 1885), Vol. I, pp. 247–265.
53. *Ibid.*, p. 315.
54. Peter Taylor Forsyth, "The Divine Self-Emptying," *God the Holy Father* (Independent Press, Ltd., London, 1957), p. 33.
55. Forsyth, *The Person and Place of Jesus Christ*, p. 303.
56. *Ibid.*, p. 310.
57. *Ibid.*, p. 336.
58. *Ibid.*, p. 353.
59. *Ibid.*, p. 357.
60. John Stewart Lawton, *Conflict in Christology* (S.P.C.K., London, 1947), p. 134.
61. William Temple, *Christus Veritas* (The Macmillan Company, London, 1949), pp. 192–193.
62. Heinrich Schumacher, *Christus in seiner Präexistenz und Kenose nach Phil. 2:5-8*, Teil I: Historische Untersuchung (Rom: Verlag des Papstl. Biblinstituts, 1914).
63. John Henry, Cardinal Newman, *Sermons Preached on Various Occasions* (Longmans, Green & Co., London, 1898), p. 87.
64. *Ibid.*, pp. 87–88.
65. *Ibid.*, p. 89.
66. *Service Book of the Orthodox Church*, tr. by I. F. Hapgood (Association Press, 1906), p. 103.
67. All the quotations from Bulgakov come from his Christological work *The Lamb of God*, originally written in Russian. There is a French translation that is a helpful guide. Gorodetzky gives some extensive English translations directly from the Russian, which I have cited here. They are found in Nadejda Gorodetzky, *The Humiliated Christ in Modern Thought* (S.P.C.K., London, 1938), p. 162.
68. *Ibid.*, pp. 165–166.
69. *Ibid.*, p. 169.
70. Søren A. Kierkegaard, *Training in Christianity*, translated by Walter Lowrie (Princeton University Press, 1941), p. 131.

71. Søren A. Kierkegaard, *Philosophical Fragments*, tr. by D. F. Swenson (Princeton University Press, 1936), p. 24.
72. Kierkegaard, *Training in Christianity*.
73. Kierkegaard, *Philosophical Fragments*, p. 25.
74. Emil Brunner, *The Christian Doctrine of Creation and Redemption, Dogmatics: Vol. II*, tr. by Olive Wyon (The Westminster Press, 1952), p. 361.
75. Karl Barth, *Church Dogmatics*, tr. by T. H. L. Parker *et al.* (T. & T. Clark, Edinburgh, 1957), Vol. II, Part 1, pp. 257 ff.
76. *Ibid.*, p. 351.
77. *Ibid.*, p. 440.
78. Karl Barth, *Church Dogmatics*, tr. by G. T. Thomson and H. Knight (Charles Scribner's Sons, 1956), Vol. I, Part 2, p. 165.
79. Karl Barth, *Church Dogmatics*, tr. by G. W. Bromiley (T. & T. Clark, Edinburgh, 1956), Vol. IV, Part 1, p. 211.

General Index

Adam, 38, 39, 40, 41
Adoptionism, 43, 63
Apollinarius, 60–61
A posteriori method, 164, 173, 175, 180, 181–184
A priori method, 164, 167, 173, 175, 180, 181–184
Aquinas, T., 145
Arianism, 29, 30, 31, 37, 56, 144, 178
Aristotelianism, Aristotle, 22, 36, 82
Athanasius, 30, 48, 56, 57, 90, 144, 145, 176, 178, 205

Barnikol, E., 35
Barth, K., 18, 21, 164–176, 180, 182, 186, 193, 202
Baur, F. C., 89, 90, 92
Behm, J., 37
Berdyaev, N., 150
Bernard of Clairvaux, 18, 20, 64–66
Biedermann, A. E., 123
Brentz, J., 74–75
Bruce, A. B., 129, 151
Brunner, E., 161–164
Bulgakov, S. N., 151–155

Calvin, J., 30, 31, 67, 71–73, 79
Celsus, 15, 16, 53, 54
Chalcedon, 48, 51, 62, 64, 151, 155, 205
Chemnitz, M., 75–76, 77, 97
Cheyne, T. K., 129

Cochrane, C. N., 49
Coinherence, 95
Communicatio idiomatum, 59, 74, 75, 77
Creed, J. M., 142
Cullmann, O., 37
Cyril of Alexandria, 58–59

Deism, 88
Deissmann, A., 32
Dibelius, O., 37
Docetism, 31, 61
Docetism, psychological, 178–179
Dorner, I. A., 91, 95, 166
Dostoevsky, F., 149

Ebrard, A., 24, 27, 91, 100–102, 130, 136
Ecumenical Councils, 23, 205–208
Ecumenical movement, 205–208
Elliott, E., 85
Enlightenment, 86–88, 104
Eschatology, 199
Exaltation, 31, 43, 45, 51, 56, 58, 63–64, 70, 78, 112, 117, 119, 138, 144, 147, 165, 174, 175, 178, 198–199
Exinanition, 70, 75, 78, 80, 147, 163

Fairbairn, A. M., 91, 130
Filaret, Metropolitan, 150–151
Formula of Concord, The, 76

Biblical Passages